A Sounding of Storytellers

A Sounding of Storytellers

New and Revised Essays on
Contemporary Writers for Children

John Rowe Townsend

J. B. Lippincott, New York

Published in Great Britain, 1979, by Kestrel Books

First published in United States of America in 1979

ISBN 0–397–31882–0

The author wishes to thank Aidan Chambers and *Signal* magazine for permission to reproduce an extract from an interview with Alan Garner, Volume 9, Number 27, September 1978.

Contents

Foreword

The present book arises out of a set of essays on leading contemporary children's writers published in 1971 under the title *A Sense of Story*. With the passage of time, *A Sense of Story* has fallen out of date. The authors who were discussed in it have produced many more books; moreover, other writers have come to the fore whom one would have wished to include. To bring all the existing essays up to date and add new ones as well would result in an impracticably bulky book. So it has seemed best to write a limited number of new essays about authors who were not previously discussed, while reworking and expanding such of the earlier studies as now seem particularly inadequate.

Of the fourteen essays which make up the present work, seven are about writers who were not in *A Sense of Story*: Nina Bawden, Vera and Bill Cleaver, Peter Dickinson, Virginia Hamilton, E. L. Konigsburg, Penelope Lively and Jill Paton Walsh. The other seven are about writers who were included in the earlier book but have moved on to new ground since I previously wrote about them: Paula Fox, Leon Garfield, Alan Garner, William Mayne, K. M. Peyton, Ivan Southall and Patricia Wrightson.

Several authors who were in *A Sense of Story* are omitted from the present book. This does not imply a lower estimate of their talents but is because I feel that what I have said about them still holds good and has not been invalidated by their more recent work. Anyone who wishes to read the essays on Joan Aiken, L. M. Boston, H. F. Brinsmead, John Christopher, Helen Cresswell, Meindert DeJong, Eleanor Estes, Madeleine L'Engle, Andre Norton, Scott O'Dell, Philippa Pearce or Rosemary Sutcliff must therefore still refer to *A Sense of Story*.

The atmosphere in which children's literature is discussed has changed since 1971. A good deal of recent comment appears to be based on the assumption that children's books are tools for shaping attitudes. Works of fiction are assessed by reference to their social context, the extent to which they deal with certain contemporary issues, and the desirability or otherwise of the views they are thought to encourage. Traditional literary values are dismissed as inappropriate or inadequate.

Actually the implication that literary criticism does not concern itself with the content of a book or with the author's attitudes is unfounded. Criticism does so concern itself, and always must. But in the present climate it is more necessary than ever to point out that there are other aspects of fiction which are also important. To look at children's books from a narrowly restricted viewpoint as means to non-literary ends is derogatory both to them and to the whole body of literature of which they form part.

In the introduction to *A Sense of Story* I said I thought there were people now writing for children who were as talented as their opposite numbers among writers for adults. (Some children's writers do indeed write for adults as well.) I explained why I believed that a critical approach to their work was called for, and how I would wish the critic's task to be performed. That introduction expresses what I still believe, and I am reprinting it here unchanged.

Cambridge, September 1978.   J.R.T.

Introduction to
A Sense of Story

This book is an introduction to the work of nineteen leading English-language writers for children. It mixes American, British and Australian writers; it includes brief biographical details and notes by the authors on themselves and their books. But mainly it consists of a set of essays in which I have tried to consider their work in literary terms.

Surveys of children's books are numerous, and so are aids to book selection, but discussion at any length of the work of individual contemporary writers is scarce. Such discussion may be thought unnecessary. I know from conversations over a period of years that there are intelligent and even bookish people to whom children's literature, by definition, is a childish thing which adults have put away. Such people may have a personal or professional interest – it is useful to have some ideas on what books to give to their children or to read to a class – but they do not pretend to be interested on their own account, and regard such an interest as an oddity, an amiable weakness. It is not my intention to quarrel with them. We cannot all be interested in everything.

Yet children are part of mankind and children's books are part of literature, and any line which is drawn to confine children or their books to their own special corner is an artificial one. Wherever the line is drawn, children and adults and books will all wander across it. Long ago *Robinson Crusoe* and *Gulliver's Travels* were adopted as children's stories. Adults have taken over *Huckleberry Finn*, argue about *Alice*, and probably enjoy *The Wind in the Willows* as much as their children do. Dickens and other Victorian novelists wrote books for the whole family; Stevenson and Rider Haggard and John Buchan and Anthony Hope wrote for boys and grown-up boys alike; and it can be offered as a pseudo-Euclidean proposition that any

9

line drawn between books for adults and books for children must pass through the middle of Kipling.

Arbitrary though it is, the division has become sharper in the present century. The main reasons have been the expansion of school and public libraries for children, and corresponding changes in the book trade. On the whole, I believe that the children's library has been a blessing to authors and publishers as well as children. The growth of a strong institutional market has eased some of the cruder commercial pressures and has made possible the writing and publication of many excellent books which otherwise could never appear. But it has hardened the dividing line between children's books and adult books into a barrier, behind which separate development now takes place.

Although the distinction is administrative rather than literary, it must have some effect on the way books are written. Yet authors are individualists, and still tend to write the book they want to write rather than one that will fit into a category. Arguments about whether such-and-such a book is 'really for children' are always cropping up, and are usually pointless in any but organizational terms. The only practical definition of a children's book today – absurd as it sounds – is 'a book which appears on the children's list of a publisher'.

Books are, in fact, continually finding their way on to the children's lists which, in another age, would have been regarded as general fiction. Abetted by their editors, writers for children constantly push out the bounds of what is acceptable. Yet because of the great division these writers, and their books, are probably more shut off than ever from the general public. (And, from this point of view, the probable growth of 'young adult' lists may raise still more fences and create new pens in which books can be trapped.) A minor reason for a book on contemporary writers for children could well be a sense of dissatisfaction with artificial barriers; a feeling that there are authors who deserve a wider public; a belief that many books which are good by any standard will now only be found by looking on the children's side of the line.

In fiction at least, the balance of talent has shifted sharply between adult books and children's books in recent years. Brian Jackson, director of the Advisory Centre for Education, in an essay on Philippa Pearce in *The Use of English* for spring 1970, declared that 'ours is the golden age of children's literature' – a view with which I agree, although the figure of speech grows wearisome – and expressed surprise that 'the great outburst of children's books this last thirty years' should come about when there is no longer a sturdy adult literature to support it. He said:

> Children's writing is a large and apparently self-contained genre, as it never was before. It is independent of the current adult novel. On the face of it, you wouldn't therefore expect its burgeoning richness. Could it be, ironically, that precisely because the adult novel is so weak in this country, some talents have been drawn into the children's field and flourished (as others have been drawn into scientific fiction and perished)?

The weakness of the current adult novel – which is not a solely British phenomenon, although it is more obvious here than in the United States – hardly needs to be demonstrated. Among much converging testimony, I draw almost at random from a few books and articles that come to hand. Anthony Burgess, in *The Novel Now*,[1] quotes Evelyn Waugh's view that 'the originators, the exuberant men, are extinct, and in their place subsists and mostly flourishes a generation notable for elegance and variety of contrivance'; and Burgess, while questioning the 'elegance' if not the 'variety of contrivance', adds on his own account: 'We cannot doubt that the twenty years since the Second World War have produced nothing to compare with the masterpieces of, say, the half-century before it.' Storm Jameson, in *Parthian Words*,[2] asks how many of us dip twice into 'the endless flow of social trivia, on its level interesting, which pours from the pens or typewriters of contemporary novelists'. The American novelist Isaac Bashevis Singer, writing in the *New York Times Book Review* on 9 November 1969, expressed the

1. *The Novel Now* (Norton, 1967; Faber, 1972).
2. *Parthian Words* (Harvill Press, 1970; Harper & Row, 1970).

belief that 'while adult literature, especially fiction, is deteriorating, the literature for children is gaining in quality and stature'. Explaining why he began to write for children in his late years, Singer declared that the child in our time

> has become a consumer of a great growing literature – a reader who cannot be deluded by literary fads and barren experiments. No writer can bribe his way to the child's attention with false originality, literary puns and puzzles, arbitrary distortions of the order of things, or muddy streams of consciousness which often reveal nothing but the writer's boring and selfish personality. I came to the child because I see in him a last refuge from a literature gone berserk and ready for suicide.

I am not sure that despair over the state of adult fiction is a good reason for becoming a writer for children. But I believe that the general picture of an ailing adult literature in contrast with a thriving literature for children is broadly correct and would be accepted by most people with knowledge of both fields. I do not mean to say that children's books are 'better' than adults', or to claim for them an excessively large place in the scheme of things. And I admit that plenty of rubbish is published for children – as indeed it is for grown-ups. But I am sure there are people writing for children today who are every bit as talented as their opposite numbers among writers for adults.

The reasons for the strength of modern fiction for children are too many and complex to be dealt with in part of a short introduction, but some of them can be hinted at. Adult fiction means, effectively, the novel. The novel is a recent form, and may be only a transitional one. Its heyday was the rapidly-changing but pre-electronic Victorian age. At present it gives the impression of shrinking into a corner: narrow, withdrawn, self-preoccupied. But children's literature has wild blood in it; its ancestry lies partly in the long ages of storytelling which preceded the novel. Myth, legend, fairy-tale are alive in their own right, endlessly reprinted, endlessly fertile in their influence. Modern children's fiction is permeated by a sense of story.

Introduction

Many writers, knowingly or unknowingly, return again and again to the old themes, often reworking them in modern or historical settings. And even where the children's novel runs parallel to its adult counterpart, there is often a freedom, speed and spontaneity which the adult novel now seems to lack.

This, I believe, is the result of an odd but happy paradox. On the one hand, most modern writers for children insist that they write, with the blessing of their editors, the books they want to write for their own satisfaction. The classic statement of this position was made by Arthur Ransome in a letter to the editor of the *Junior Bookshelf* as long ago as 1937: 'You write not for children but for yourself, and if, by good fortune, children enjoy what you enjoy, why then, you are a writer of children's books . . . No special credit to you, but simply thumping good luck.' C. S. Lewis said[3] that the only reason why he would ever write for children was 'because a children's story is the best art form for something you have to say'; he also remarked that 'I am almost inclined to set it up as a canon that a children's story which is enjoyed only by children is a bad children's story'. Yet anyone writing a book that will appear on a children's list must be aware of a potential readership of children. This is the fruitful contradiction from which the children's writer benefits. However much he is writing for himself he must, consciously or unconsciously, have a special sense of audience. As Arthur Ransome, rightly unworried by any inconsistency, went on to say in the letter already quoted: 'Every writer wants to have readers, and than children there are no better readers in the world.'

An author can – as I have said elsewhere – expect from the reading child as much intelligence, as much imagination, as from the grown-up, and a good deal more readiness to enter into things and live the story. He can take up his theme afresh as if the world were new, rather than picking it up where the last practitioner let it drop and allowing for the weariness and satiety of his readers. He cannot expect children to put up with

3. 'Three Ways of Writing for Children' in *Only Connect* (ed. Sheila Egoff, O.U.P., Canada 1969).

long-windedness or pomposity or emperors' clothes; but that is a discipline rather than a restriction. True, the child's range of experience is limited. There are still some kinds of book that are not likely to appear on the children's list: not because they will corrupt a child but because they will bore him. But, in general, children and their books are much less inhibited now than they were in Arthur Ransome's day. In my experience, children's writers do not feel much hampered; mostly they are able to do what they want to do. They are fortunate people. Their sense on the one hand of scope and freedom, on the other of a constantly-renewed and responsive readership, freshens their work and makes this an exhilarating sector to be concerned with.

Nevertheless, children's books need to be appraised with coolness and detachment, simple enthusiasm being little better than simple unawareness. A critical approach is desirable not only for its own sake but also as a stimulus and discipline for author and publisher, and – in the long run – for the improvement of the breed. This indeed is the strongest reason for it. Donnarae MacCann, introducing a series of articles in the *Wilson Library Bulletin* for December 1969, quoted from Henry S. Canby's *Definitions*: 'Unless there is somewhere an intelligent critical attitude against which the writer can measure himself . . . one of the chief requirements for good literature is wanting . . . The author degenerates.'

In the United States and Britain, the positions of writers for children in the league-table are well-known among specialists in the field; possibly too well-known. But, as Donnarae Mac-Cann says, 'there is no body of critical writing to turn to, even for those books which have been awarded the highest literary prizes in children's literature in Britain and America'. Of the authors discussed in this book, only a few have been the subject of any sustained critical appraisal. The children's writer, when his work begins to make any impression, can expect his new book to get a few reviews: some by specialists with much knowledge but little critical acumen, some by non-specialists with – presumably – critical acumen but not much knowledge

Introduction

of children's books, some by people with no obvious qualifications at all. With luck the book may be reviewed in two or three places by critics who can place it in its context and can exercise some worthwhile judgement; but they are unlikely to have much space in which to work. And reviewing, even at its best, is a special and limited form of criticism: a rapid tasting rather than a leisurely consideration.

Mention of the criticism of children's books will usually lead to an argument about the relevance of various criteria. It seems to me that it is perfectly possible to judge books for children by non-literary standards. It is legitimate to consider the social or moral or psychological or educational impact of a book; to consider how many children, and what kind of children, will like it. But it is dangerous to do this and call it criticism. Most disputes over standards are fruitless because the antagonists suppose their criteria to be mutually exclusive; if one is right the other must be wrong. This is not necessarily so. Different kinds of assessment are valid for different purposes. The important thing is that everyone should understand what is being done.

The critic who is concerned with a book as literature cannot, however, carry his 'standards' around with him like a set of tools ready for any job. He should, I believe, approach a book with an open mind and respond to it as freshly and honestly as he is able; then he should go away, let his thoughts and feelings about it mature, turn them over from time to time, consider the book in relation to others by the same author and by the author's predecessors and contemporaries. If the book is for children he should not let his mind be dominated by the fact; but neither, I think, should he attempt to ignore it. Myself – as one who remembers being a child, has children of his own, and has written for children – I could not, even if I wished, put children out of my mind when reading books intended for them. Just as the author must, I believe, write for himself yet with awareness of an audience of children, so the critic must write for himself with an awareness that the books he discusses are books written for children.

But this awareness should not, I think, be too specific. Neither author nor critic should be continually asking himself questions such as: 'Will this be comprehensible to the average eleven-year-old?' We all know there is no average child. Children are individuals, and will read books if they like them and when they are ready for them. A suggestion that a book may appeal to a particular age-group or type of child can be helpful, especially in reviews, but it should always be tentative and it should not affect one's assessment of merit. It has always seemed clear to me that a good book for children must be a good book in its own right. And a book can be good without being immensely popular and without solving its readers' problems or making them kinder to others.

It may seem that in these remarks about the criticism of children's literature I am by implication making highflown claims for the book that follows. It is not so. I am fully aware of my shortcomings. In saying what I think can and should be done, I am not suggesting that I have done it. And the dual aim of introducing writers to a wider public and addressing myself seriously to their work has set some problems of its own. Nineteen authors may seem a small number to pick out from all the talented people now writing for children in English, but is quite a large number for one person to study. To be properly equipped to write a 2,000-word essay on an author, one should be qualified to write a whole book on him, for the knowledge and understanding required are no less. I know all too well that I have not qualified myself to write nineteen books.

The writers included here are not presented with any claim that they are 'the best'. Every reader with knowledge of the field will be irritated, if not outraged, by my omissions, and probably by some of my inclusions. Everyone will feel that some writers who are left out are better than some who are in. I would not try to deny it. I have chosen on a personal basis. These are authors whose work particularly interests me and about whom I feel I have something to say. There have, however, been factors at work other than purely individual inclination. 'Contemporary' is a key word in the selection; I have chosen writers who are alive and active at the time of going to press. I

Introduction

have tried to produce a reasonable mixture of American, Australian and British authors while confining myself to those whose work is known and available in all three countries. This causes no injustice to British or Australian writers, for American publishers are assiduous in seeking out and buying rights in their work; but it is hard on some good American writers whose work is unknown or little-known over here. The temptation to list authors whom I should have liked to include, but for one reason or another could not, is strong but must be resisted. It could not make the process of selection less invidious.

My thanks are due to all the publishers who have helped me with books and information, and to all the authors who have been kind enough either to write specially for me about themselves and their work or to give permission for the use of extracts from lectures and articles. It will be seen that their contributions differ a good deal from each other. This is because of differences in my own approaches to them. I did not ask, or want, them all to do the same thing. If the resulting variety is a fault – though I do not think it is – the blame is mine.

Knutsford, July 1971   J.R.T.

Nina Bawden

Nina Bawden was born in London in 1925 and was educated at Somerville College, Oxford. She was elected a Fellow of the Royal Society of Literature in 1970. She has three children, and lives in London. Nina Bawden has written sixteen novels for adults, and her books for children include A Handful of Thieves *(1967),* Carrie's War *(1973) and* Rebel on a Rock *(1978). She received the* Guardian *Award for* The Peppermint Pig *(1975).*

The mother of Kate Pollack, in Nina Bawden's book *Squib* (1971), is an illustrator; and in an early chapter Kate stands beside her, looking at a drawing of frightened children in a wood. 'What are they scared of?' Kate asks. 'I don't know yet,' says her mother. 'I haven't finished reading the book. . . You see, they don't know what they're frightened of, at this point in the story. So it's best I don't know either. You get a truer feeling, that way.'

Near the end of the book, Kate remembers this reply and asks her mother what was frightening in the wood. 'Oh, robbers, buried treasure, that sort of thing,' says Mother. 'Not much sense to it, really.'

In their context, this question and answer are very much to the point. Kate herself has been confusing fiction with reality. *Squib* is about children who come across an ill-treated child, don't understand what is going on and devise fanciful explanations; but when one of the children sees Squib's face and hands pressed flat against the window of the old bus in which he is kept locked up, she knows she has seen 'something more frightening than a hundred old witches'. And so she has, of course; the ill-treatment of children by the adults who are supposed to look after them comes close to being the ultimate terror of childhood. In comparison, 'robbers, buried treasure, that sort of thing' are trivial: mere clichés of children's fiction which may encourage self-deception. One agrees with Kate's mother that there is 'not much sense to it', but can hardly help remembering that the early books for children of Nina Bawden herself did rather tend to go in for 'that sort of thing'. Secret passages, trappings in caves, outwitting of plotters, exposure of jewel thieves, pursuit of a crook by children: these and other ingredients of the standard adventure story can all be found in the half-dozen books by Nina Bawden which preceded *Squib*.

There is of course nothing wrong with adventure as such. Nina Bawden herself remarked in 1972 that she aimed to put before children

what I hope are exciting adventure stories in a world that is real to them, and include situations and feelings they know. Adventure stories are important to children, not just the what-happens-next excitement, but because they can see themselves taking part in the action and test themselves: would they be brave in such a situation, or would they run away? Few children have a chance to do this in real life.[1]

This makes excellent sense. Yet surely the contrived adventure of the conventional children's story does not achieve such an aim; it is unreal, an escape, a kind of fantasy. And it was evident from the beginning that Nina Bawden – already an established novelist when her first children's book appeared – had more to offer than this. In adult novels she had written with extraordinary insight and sensitivity about childhood and about relationships between children and adults. It was not surprising that she should turn to writing for children; it was only surprising that she should be content with such hackneyed plot devices. One may guess that she began, consciously or unconsciously, with a

1. Nina Bawden, address to National Book League conference in Birmingham, November 1972, reported in *Signal* 11, May 1973, p. 106.

restrictive image of what constituted an acceptable children's story, and that this image has gradually been reshaped. In *Squib,* and in the two wholly admirable books which followed it, *Carrie's War* (1973) and *The Peppermint Pig* (1975), the situations are realistic and the adventures arise naturally out of the characters and background. And this does not make them less exciting, less appealing to children, or less suitable for identification and the testing of oneself in hypothetical circumstances. Quite the reverse, in fact.

It should be said at once that, whatever their faults, there are some very good things in those early books. In the first of them, *The Secret Passage* (1963), John and Mary and above all outrageous seven-year-old Ben are perfectly real and credible children; the opening chapters, which tell of the events that led to their coming home from Kenya, are strong and graphic; and a theme which underlies the book and is beautifully handled is that of the children's adjustment to life in England with the apparently forbidding but in reality warm and loving Aunt Mabel. Yet there is a great deal that is at once improbable and commonplace. Pale, pinched, disagreeable Victoria, whom the children find in the house at the other end of that secret passage, is a brilliant pianist; sour old Mr Reynolds, who keeps his art treasures shut away and proclaims the children to be 'a parcel of thieving brats', becomes Victoria's benefactor and also buys the sculpture of amiable red-haired giant artist 'Uncle' Abe Agnew; apparently-penniless aged eccentric Miss Pin is really a rich woman and makes Ben her heir; and the book ends conventionally with 'the best thing of all' – Dad arriving home from Africa.

In other early books there are similar uneasy mixtures of fictional cliché with the 'world that is real to children and the situations and feelings they know'. In *On the Run* (1964), Ben, now eleven, meets (by the accident of the way a ball happens to bounce) Thomas, the son of a threatened East African Premier, and Lil, a waif who is a refugee from the Welfare; and they all run away together, facing and escaping various dangers and thwarting a plot against Thomas's father. Ben's talents for

Nina Bawden

observation from tree branches, a fire escape, and other hidden vantage points come in handy; and when the children are caught by the tide in a cave they are resourceful, agile, and conveniently equipped with a rope up which to escape. *The Witch's Daughter* (1966) brings to a Scottish island Mr Smith and Mr Jones, a remarkably inept pair of jewel robbers who have been waiting for the furore to die down before disposing of their loot. Children, naturally, help to bring them to book, just as in *A Handful of Thieves* (1967) children track down the confidence trickster who has robbed an old lady.

Yet the children in these early books live and breathe; they speak like real children, react as one would expect real children to react, and are seen in developing relationships with each other and with the grown-ups around them. Could it be argued on the author's behalf that she is managing to have it both ways – to keep her young readers turning the page while giving them more than they realize they are getting? I think it could; but one must face the fact that the quiet verisimilitude of the characters and relationships makes improbable events all the more improbable. There is a good example in *The Runaway Summer* (1969), an intermediate book, and probably Nina Bawden's best for children up to that time. Here two children harbour a young illegal immigrant. But one doesn't really believe they *would*; they are quite a responsible pair – one is a policeman's son – and they would surely have sought adult help. Children have a strong sense of what situations they can and cannot cope with on their own. In a different kind of story, far more exotic events could be accepted without the slightest hesitation; but in this generally realistic novel, credibility is strained. In *Squib*, *Carrie's War* and *The Peppermint Pig*, the gap at last is closed. The discovery of an ill-treated small boy; the experiences of Carrie and younger brother Nick during wartime evacuation to Wales; the Greengrass family's year in rural Norfolk while Father is away: these stories show children in believable circumstances, doing what children might reasonably be expected to do, and the compulsion to turn the page is as strong as ever. Nina Bawden has solved the problem of the realistic writer for children: not by 'having it both ways' but by achieving a single, unified appeal of action, characters and situation.

Nina Bawden's children are defined by their responses and relationships: hardly ever by description. She does not explain that Carrie is a careful, conscientious, worrying kind of child; but we see Carrie trying to cope with the small stratagems of adult life, embarrassed by younger brother Nick and seeking to prevent him from behaving outrageously; and we may or may not notice that sometimes the responsible Carrie does the wrong thing while irresponsible Nick gets it right. There is never a trace of sentimentality. Janey in *The Witch's Daughter* is blind, but she is not presented as an object for sympathy. She is a talkative little girl of marked idiosyncrasy; and when she has helped sighted children out of the blackness of a cave she is full of her own achievement:

'It was terribly clever of me,' she said admiringly, after she had told the story for the second time. 'If it hadn't been for me, we would have been skeletons by now, I expect, just our poor bones lying there, like the sheep skulls. I was a heroine, wasn't I, Perdita?'

Mary, in *The Runaway Summer,* goes to London to look for the uncle of her small immigrant and fails to find him, but rescues her cat from her parents' former flat; and before the day is over, she is so full of the recovery of the cat that she has practically forgotten her original mission. In *The Peppermint Pig,* the remark of the cottage child Annie that 'there's always plenty to eat, pig-killing time' makes its own, sufficient statement about a rural child's poverty. The five children in *A Handful of Thieves* are individuals as well as members of a gang, and are illuminated by small, precise sidelights: Clio, for instance, hates to apologize, and when told to do so 'went off on her own, wandering over the dump and kicking at the rubbish'.

Younger children are generally seen from an older child's point of view, and are among Nina Bawden's most successful characterizations. In *The Secret Passage*, the show is constantly being stolen by Ben, the dreadful seven-year-old, forthright and articulate but not yet old enough for tact and responsibility. When Ben reappears in *On the Run*, now aged eleven, he is less interesting, perhaps because he is now cast as the 'viewpoint character', whom the reader can imagine to be himself. The Cockney waif Lil is the most memorable person in this book. Polly-Anna, the diminutive twins in *The Runaway Summer*, and Sammy and Prue in *Squib*, are other small children who are lightly but accurately sketched. So far as I can recall, there is only one glimpse in all the books up to *The Peppermint Pig* of a person growing out of childhood. This is in *The White Horse Gang* (1966), a mid-career book about a group of children whose exploits include the kidnapping of another child. One of the group is Abe, and at the end he fails to appear at school for several days and is then found by the other children driving a farm tractor. He speaks briefly to them, then says he must get on with the job; and his manner, friendly but distant, opens up a gulf. He is doing a man's work, is not a child any more, and though the children talk of forming another gang next year it is clear that things will never be the same again. We have come to the frontiers of childhood. Over there lies another country.

Yet while staying at this side of the border, Nina Bawden is well aware of the depth and fullness of a child's emotions. In this context an extended comparison of the approaches to childhood in her adult and in her children's books would be illuminating. That is impossible in the space of the present essay. Briefly it may be said that while children in the adult books – Emmie in *Tortoise by Candlelight*,[2] for instance, or Lucy in *The Birds on the Trees*[3] – are seen sympathetically and as if from within, one is nevertheless presented with a view of their thoughts and feelings that is appropriate to an adult audience. It is a view, as it were, simultaneously from inside and at an adult distance. Not that Nina Bawden makes the mistake of supposing that adults can always understand children: she is much concerned with the fact that frequently they cannot, and in *Tortoise by Candlelight* there is a dry reference to the 'simple

2. *Tortoise by Candlelight* (Longman, 1963; Queens House, 1976).
3. *The Birds on the Trees* (Longman, 1970; Harper & Row, 1971).

adult mind' of the man next door who is trying in vain to fathom the complexities of the desperately over-strained Emmie.

In the children's books there is some simplification, and I think some omission, but nothing is falsified, and Nina Bawden does not shrink from the portrayal of grief and pain. Kate in *Squib* and Mary in *The Runaway Summer* have suffered real psychological damage – Kate through the drowning of her father and brother, Mary through the breakup of her parents' marriage – and the direct and indirect effects can be seen clearly in what they say and do. When for instance Mary is telling her friend Simon of the agony she is in, for fear that her Aunt Alice will find out that she has been romancing about having a cruel aunt, there suddenly bursts out, uncontrollably, the greater agony of feeling unloved and deserted by her parents. But there are also depths of positive emotion, as when Carrie, while in Wales as an evacuee, feels wildly happy, sings to herself along the railway track, and goes 'hop, skip and jump down the hilly street' and through the shop door with laughter bubbling up inside her.

Alas, Carrie has forgotten that it's a mistake to let the mean-spirited Mr Evans, the shopkeeper on whom she and Nick are billeted, see that she is happy, and he soon takes it out of her. But that is another matter. Nina Bawden knows very well that it's tough being a child in a world run by and for adults. You are so much at adult mercy, people won't take you seriously, you are ignored or pushed around. 'It's a fearful handicap being a child,' Carrie says elsewhere. 'You have to stand there and watch, you can never make anything happen.' Adults are immensely important to children, even if they hardly appear to notice a child unless it annoys them. Children do of course have to cope with the adult world; sometimes they cannot tell what the adults are getting at, but other times they see through them more than the adults realize, and they exploit such advantages as they have. It can be quite a help to be unnoticed when you don't *want* to be noticed.

Besides being a shrewd analyst of child–adult politics, Nina

Nina Bawden

Bawden is outstandingly good at assessing adults from a child's point of view. In dealing with adults she is willing to allow straightforward, sensible values to emerge. She is charitable about the dowdy, the shy, the unattractive, the not-very-bright. The only adults she shows in a consistently harsh light are the snobbish, pretentious and affected, and the smooth colour-supplement people. There is a chilling picture in *Squib* of the trendy young mother Sophie, who exploits Kate's willingness to look after her baby but doesn't bother to go and see her when she is in hospital; and there's an enlightening contrast with the splendid Mrs Tite, Kate's mother's help, who runs a sizeable family with cheerful efficiency. 'When the Tite children swam in the sea their mother was always beside them, a floating tank, a human lifebelt.' This tiny vignette surely symbolizes the reliance of children on adults, the need for assurance, the parental obligation.

The adult character one loves to hate is mean Mr Evans in *Carrie's War*. His is the most highly coloured portrait in the later and better Bawden books, but it never ceases to carry conviction, and it gives openings for occasional quiet humour. 'Up and down the stairs, soon as my back's turned, wearing out the stair carpet,' Mr Evans complains of the children; and (without the slightest intention of joking) 'No rest for the righteous!' But even Mr Evans, the self-made man who survived a hard childhood, is seen with some sympathy. When 'Auntie Lou', his downtrodden sister, leaves to be married, he takes refuge, pathetically, in his own meanness: ' "Ate a lot, your Auntie Lou did. Always at it, munch munch, nibble nibble, just like a rabbit. Now she's gone, there'll be one less mouth to feed." ' Yet we learn that not long afterwards Mr Evans died: 'Heart, the doctors said, but it was more grief and loneliness. Missed his sister. . .'

The view of grown-ups is usually a child's-eye view, and is confined to the aspects that are relevant for the book. But it is clear that the rest of adult life is there. Sometimes a quite different novel could be written on the same situation from an adult viewpoint, and one knows that Nina Bawden could write it. The story of the Greengrass family in *The Peppermint Pig*, hard up in rural Norfolk while Father, having quixotically given up his job, goes off to try his luck in America (and obviously doesn't succeed), would be very different if told from the point of view of the children's mother.

There is quite a lot of death and illness in Nina Bawden's books; and there are gruesome incidents like the loss of Granny Greengrass's finger at the butcher's, as well as sad but necessary ones like the fate of Johnnie, the pig himself, who must in the end go the way of all fat pigs. Nina Bawden clearly has a realistic and sensible view of what children can take. Squib, the ill-treated small boy in the book of that name, is seen from a distance; we are never told how he feels or, directly, what is happening to him. To have written about Squib himself, as Nina Bawden has said, would have been too horrifying and also morally confusing, since 'one would have had to consider the ignorant foster mother and her stupid husband'.[4] It may be noted that the decision to keep Squib's own consciousness out of the picture was carried out, and had to be carried out, with perfect consistency. If Squib had spoken a single word – which he never does – the perspective would have been different. And some highly professional craftsmanship was needed in order to avoid producing any situation in which Squib would have to speak.

But then, Nina Bawden *is* a fine craftsman; and she has that particular excellence of craftsmanship whose hallmark is its unobtrusiveness. A perfect join is an unnoticeable join. She knows how to organize material, begin and end a chapter, keep a story moving, sustain interest; she does not go in for spectacular effects. There are many neat touches in her work, such as the placing of the story of *Carrie's War* in the framework of Carrie's return years later, thus bringing it into contact with the present; and the fact that Carrie's children are not named. This last small decision, though not obvious, is quite right. The main story is set in the time of Carrie's childhood; to give the names of her

4. Nina Bawden, address to National Book League conference in Birmingham, November 1972, reported in *Signal* 11, May 1973, p. 106.

own children would be to introduce unnecessary and possibly confusing detail into the outer frame.

Carrie's children are named, however, in *Rebel on a Rock* (1978), Nina Bawden's newest book, which has just been published at the time of writing. The widowed Carrie has married Albert Sandwich, who appeared as a boy in the earlier book, and has brought with her Charlie and Jo, aged fourteen and twelve, and two small black adopted children, Alice and James. This story, told by Jo, seems at first sight a reversion to the earlier adventure novels; but it is a reversion with a subtle difference. In a country closely resembling Greece, the family, and Jo in particular, are involved in the outer edges of a plan to remove the dictator. But not only do they not forward the plan; they unwittingly give it away, causing it to collapse and a brave man to be arrested. This is, in realistic terms, the most likely result of children's intervention in such matters, but it runs totally and originally counter to the tradition of the children's story. For that very reason it could possibly disappoint some young readers, but it should certainly make them think. Nina Bawden's understanding of the strains in a family where there is a stepfather, however amiable, and her grasp of the psychology of children on the verge of adolescence, are as shrewd and sympathetic as one would expect.

Children probably have a subliminal sense of the personality of their authors, and I have no doubt that the Nina Bawden who can be sensed behind all her books is sensible, understanding, kind but not soppy, and at times healthily down-to-earth. She does not write for effect, and her unpretentious use of words does not proclaim its own merits or lend itself to quotation. Her books are her style. Yet again and again her writing is perfect for its purpose. The ending of *The Peppermint Pig* is as good an instance as any. This has really been the story of how the Greengrass family got along while Father was away; Johnnie the pig is only a part of it; but he is the part that comes first to Poll Greengrass's mind when Father returns, looking for a moment like a stranger, and asking her what has been happening to her.

She tried to think. So much – but she could only remember one thing. A little pig, sitting in a pint beer mug and squealing. A bigger pig, trotting behind Mother when she went shopping. A naughty pig, stealing Hot Cross Buns and next door's gooseberries. A famous pig, the talk of the Town, sitting good as gold in the drawing-room of the Manor House with his head in his hostess's lap. A portly pig, snoozing on the doorstep in the sun. . .

Johnnie, the peppermint pig, gone now like this whole, long year of her life, but fixed and safe in her mind, for ever and ever.

She said, 'Johnnie's dead.'

Father looked at her, puzzled, but smiling. He cupped her chin in his hand and said, 'My darling, who's Johnnie?'

Nina Bawden

Nina Bawden writes:

Children, as Henry James knew, are very *useful* to a novelist who wants to comment on the follies of adult society. Children inhabit the same world but they look at it differently. You can use a child's eyes, his innocence and fresh susceptibilities, to challenge accepted assumptions, to separate the genuine from the hypocritical.

I used children for this purpose in my adult novels – *Tortoise by Candlelight* and *Devil by the Sea*[1] – long before I thought of writing a children's book. But writing *about* children, I found I remembered my own childhood so clearly – how I had felt, what I had suffered, the things I had laughed at – that to write *for* them seemed a natural development.

Nowadays I write a novel for adults one year, a novel for children the next, and I find that one kind of book 'feeds' the other. Writing about children, you ponder on what will happen to them when they are grown; writing about adults, you need to know what they once were. The story of *Squib,* for example, about an ill-treated child and the children who rescue him, gave me the theme for *Anna Apparent,*[2] an adult novel about the effects of that kind of experience in childhood on an apparently 'normal' young woman.

The things I write about for adults, I write about for children, too: emotions, motives, the difficulties of being honest with oneself, the gulf between what people say and what they really mean. All the levels are there, the 'whole story'. The only differences, apart from minor adjustments of style – you cannot be too allusive for children because they know less than we do – are ones of emphasis, and interest, and viewpoint. When I write for adults, I am writing with an adult perspective, about the way life looks to me from where I stand now. When I write for children, I am writing from the point of view of the child who still lurks inside me, still hopeful, still trusting, who sees the world as a place that is potentially full of exciting adventure and who likes to tell, and be told, a good tale about it.

1. *Devil by the Sea* (Collins, 1957; Lippincott, 1976).
2. *Anna Apparent* (Longman, 1972).

Vera and Bill Cleaver

Vera Cleaver was born in South Dakota, and her husband Bill in Seattle, Washington. They were married in 1945 but did not begin their joint writing career until 1967, when the publication of Ellen Grae *immediately established their position among the leading American writers for young people. The books that followed have reinforced this position; they include* Where the Lilies Bloom *(1969),* Grover *(1970),* The Whys and Wherefores of Littabelle Lee *(1973) and* Trial Valley *(1977). The Cleavers now live in Winter Haven, Florida.*

Sleepy and ill-humoured, shivering with the cold, they would shamble out and set their feet one in front of the other and we would start off down the valley, the wagon in tow, the wheels of it creaking and rattling with every step and turn. I would try to get them to sing or talk, do anything to raise their spirits, but they remained sullenly silent. At that hour they hated me and I hated myself, knowing how I appeared to them – a pinch-faced crone, straggle-haired, bony, ragged, too desperate for anyone with only fourteen years on them but still driven by a desperation that was unholy and ugly. Straggling up the mountainside through the sodden, gloomy daybreak I would see the beauty of it all around me, free for the looking and the listening. Surely, I would think, the Lord is here. Roy Luther believed that he was and I believe it, too. He is here and watching over everything, helping it. I believe that. But if this is so where is my share of the help, answer me that. There isn't going to be any help for me, is there? There's just going to be me and this mountain and that other one over there and these three children and whatever good we can make for ourselves.

There is no mistaking either the content or the tone of voice. These could only be the words of the heroine of a novel by Vera and Bill Cleaver. Listen again.

Vera and Bill Cleaver

When was it all of this took place? Oh, not so long ago, and yet long ago, when I was sixteen and had not yet learned to take notice of time. I heard no knell for the departed months and years; there were so many ahead. I had not discovered everything in myself or yet even half of it. What was there to discover? When a person, simple and childlike in nature, looks in his mirror, he doesn't expect to see the image of a great thinker look back. And a good thing too.

Until I turned sixteen, I went to school during the fall and winter months and sat at a desk, learning a few facts about the world. In the summers I was a sweet roamer. Sometimes I would go with my Aunt Sorrow to the woods to gather medicine plants or ride into the back hills with her to see after a patient; she was a nature doctor.

The first speaker is Mary Call Luther, from *Where the Lilies Bloom* (1969); the second is Littabelle, from *The Whys and Wherefores of Littabelle Lee* (1973). It is a rather formal English, falling roundly and well on the ear; not quite Biblical in tone, but with echoes perhaps of the voice of the preacher, interspersed now and then with the short, sharp, down-to-earth comment: 'There isn't going to be any help for me, is there?' or 'And a good thing too.' It is the expression in each case of a formidable personality: indomitable, self-reliant, responsible, proud and with a proper sense of its own worth, and, for all that, young.

Rereading the Cleavers' books for children – a dozen of them up to the time of writing – one is struck most obviously and forcibly by their gallery of fierce, determined heroines like Mary Call and Littabelle; by their vividly drawn settings in Allegheny or Ozark mountain country, in Florida small town or Dakota badland; and by the ordeals their young people have to face. Like the Australian writer Ivan Southall, with whom they have little else in common, the Cleavers tend to put their central characters into situations which are at or beyond the limits of what they can cope with. In their first book, *Ellen Grae* (1967), Ellen has to carry an insupportable burden of knowledge about the deaths of her friend Ira's parents. Grover, in the book named after him, has a mother who is dying of cancer and who kills herself to shorten the agony. In *Where the Lilies Bloom*,

A Sounding of Storytellers

Mary Call Luther struggles to keep together a parentless family of four, including 'cloudy-headed' older sister Devola, while they scratch a precarious living by gathering wild plants among the mountains. Annie Jelks in *I Would Rather be a Turnip* (1971) is oppressed by small-town censoriousness over the illegitimate child in her family. Intelligent Lydia, in *Me Too* (1973), has not merely to live with her mentally-handicapped, unresponsive twin Lornie after their father has had enough and decamped; she feels she must try to improve Lornie's behaviour and to teach her when the special school has failed. Littabelle looks after her aged grandparents in desperate circumstances when their house has burned down, winter is coming, and their children refuse to support them. Other characters face difficulties hardly less daunting.

The Cleaver novels are rooted in an unyielding realism. No wind is tempered to the shorn lamb; no rich uncle or equivalent turns up with infusions of love and money; no dying parent recovers or absconding one returns repentant. Real life probably contains more happy accidents, more unexpected bonuses, more merciful softening of harsh situations than the Cleavers ever permit themselves. The circumstances of each story assert themselves ruthlessly and dictate the solution. While some of the protagonists win through, others are defeated. Lydia can do little or nothing for sister Lornie; the Proffitts in *The Mimosa Tree* (1970) can find no way to survive in a Chicago slum; Ussy Mock in *The Mock Revolt* (1971) cannot escape from his small-town ambience and his own sense of responsibility.

Yet the overall impression left by individual books and by the Cleavers' work as a whole is not a depressing one. The fight must be fought, but if the end is defeat, very well then, the end is defeat and there is no disgrace in it. It is better to have fought and lost than not to have fought. Lydia realizes at the end of *Me Too* that 'in failure there is certainty and in certainty there is release'. And though there is self-sacrifice in the Cleaver novels, sometimes on a heroic scale, there is also the recognition that even the most self-sacrificing people have a duty to themselves. Lydia must save herself from being dragged down by Lornie, just as she must save herself from the sinkhole that opens up beneath her in the scrub. Littabelle in *The Whys and Wherefores* and Mary Call at the end of *Trial Valley* (1977; the sequel to *Where the Lilies Bloom*) are determined to overcome their ignorance, get some education and make something of their own lives; and having seen them in action we know that nothing can stop them.

This sense of the indomitability of the human spirit is undoubtedly the major reason why in the end the Cleaver books are more likely to lift up than cast down the reader, to offer an astringent yet stimulating experience. There is also a strong minor reason, in that wry humour, salty dialogue and intriguing surface incident are counterpointed against the grave underlying themes. Ellen Grae is a teller of tall tales which are often extremely funny, as are her conversations with friend Grover and room-mate Rosemary. In *Grover* (1970), the adventures of Grover and Ellen Grae while delivering telegrams, and the comedy of their being outwitted by small boy Farrell, occupy the foreground during the time in which Grover is coming to realize that his mother will die. Light incidents such as these do nothing to diminish the seriousness of the book, but they save it from being constantly harrowing, and they give all the more force to moments such as the one when, after a day on the river, Grover lies awake at night and says aloud to himself that his mother is going to die; 'testing the words for the truth that was in them and hearing it there'.

The Cleaver heroines, though bearing a family likeness to each other, are clearly distinguishable (with the possible exceptions of Mary Call and Littabelle, who chime very closely together). Ellen Grae is a bright imaginative eccentric, Mary Call and Littabelle are dourly practical, Delpha in *Delpha Green and Company* (1972) is a lively extrovert who changes the lives of those around her. Annie Jelks, in *I Would Rather be a Turnip*, oppressed by small-town censoriousness, is a particularly memorable character. Annie is bad-tempered and unlikeable, and bitter in her resentment of the harmless illegitimate child who provokes this censoriousness; but she is a true Cleaver heroine all the same, and by the end, when she has crossly saved Calvin's life and rudely rejected his thanks, one finds oneself liking and even admiring this graceless character; one knows that her loyalty to Calvin, her family, or anyone she accepted as a friend would be grudging but unbounded.

One would infer from the Cleaver novels that women are the stronger sex: a correct inference, in my view, and for the same reason in the books as in life. Women are stronger because coping makes them so. 'Men, God pity them, are such poor sticks,' says Mary Call, and there are some feeble men in these books. Roy Luther, Mary Call's father, cannot help it that he is dying, but even in health he doesn't seem to have done much to win a decent life for his family. Grover's father goes to pieces when his wife dies, and it is the black housekeeper Rose who keeps things going. There are other portraits of weak and unsatisfactory men, though it would be wrong to suggest that the Cleavers are anti-male sexists. Grover himself comes through his ordeal: he is solid, strong, reliable, he aims to be a veterinarian when he grows up, and one knows that he will be a good one. Lydia, in *Me Too*, suffers from attempts at ostracism by people who think her sister's mental deficiency may run in her family, but her friend Billy Frank is firmly loyal to her: 'We're friends,' he says, 'and can't nobody stop us.'

Apart from Grover, Ussy Mock in *The Mock Revolt* is the Cleavers' only male central character so far. One can hardly call him a hero, he isn't even particularly impressive; but he wins respect and – a very Cleaverlike touch – his own self-respect. Ussy, trying to save up money to get away from the 'deadlies' in his small town, finds himself supporting the deadweight of Luke Wilder and his hopeless family. The demands of the Wilders consume Ussy's hard-earned vacation pay; the escape dream fades. It is borne in on Ussy that, in the words of the novelist W. M. Thackeray, 'dependence is a perpetual call on humanity'. He doesn't even *like* Luke, but Luke is there; and roaring off on a motorbike to New Orleans and San Francisco is not an option that is open to Ussy. For all his wish to be different, he knows that one day he will be a little baggy old man like those he sees in the town, trotting around his garden with a watering-can.

Of villainy in the traditional sense there is none in the Cleaver novels, but there is some brute ignorance, and there is the mental cruelty of those who will make young people suffer for an illegitimate or backward sibling or a parent who shot herself. And there is the cold selfishness of Hutchens, Ora and Estie in *Littabelle Lee,* who leave their aged parents to sink or swim. (It is a fine, all too realistic touch that when Littabelle brings an action on the old people's behalf and wins support for them from their defaulting children, they are totally ungrateful and consider it a disgrace.)

I have heard it suggested that there are passages in these books that are too gruesome to be suitable for children: the description, for instance, of Littabelle's help to a woman who is giving birth without medical or nursing care, or her operation on the windpipe of a choking child, carried out with a penknife. Gratuitous horrors are, I think, always bad art, and in a children's book are morally objectionable; but there is of course an opposite error of falsely smoothing the rough edges of life, and to me it seems that when the Cleavers shock they do so almost invariably for good reasons and within current tolerances. There is much in the account of mentally-handicapped Lornie's behaviour in *Me Too* which makes painful reading, but which surely is required for the honest treatment of the theme. This book has a fearful and unforgettable moment at the end when Lornie, returned at last to her special school, re-encounters her fellow-pupil Jane, who has been mentioned from time to time in the narrative but has never appeared.

Lornie left off her shuffling and was standing still with her head raised. A door was opening, ever so slowly, and Lornie turned towards it, watching. She licked her teeth and her hand went to her necklaces.

A figure stood in the door. It had mop-hair, the colour of old dust, which set a stage for a young-old face. Its smile was a child's. Its eyes did not belong to childhood nor yet to the state of adults. They belonged to that yet unsettled state where Lornie and all like Lornie lived.

The figure in the door said, 'Yer. Lornie.'

And Lornie, running forward, said, 'Yerrrrrrr. Janie.'

They flung their arms around each other and hugged.

In all the twelve books, the one passage that troubles me is the description in graphic detail of how Grover, taking bloody revenge on a woman who tormented him over his mother's death, kills her turkey by chopping off its head. I am not convinced of the artistic necessity or psychological accuracy of this; and, if it is unnecessary, it is pointless and repellent violence.

Settings are of great importance in the Cleaver novels. Trial Valley, in the Appalachian mountain country, is 'fair land, the fairest of them all'; and through all the tribulations of the Luther family, this landscape in which and on which they live is never lost sight of. Ellen Grae deeply loves the small Florida town of Thicket – 'day after sunny day and night after starlit night Thicket is as neat and as beautiful as a rose garden' – and an unsuccessful attempt to take her away from it is the principal material of *Lady Ellen Grae* (1968). The South Dakota badlands, in *Dust of the Earth* (1975), bring to Fern Drawn's mind 'a picture of an old, lost royal city I have never seen'.

Covering an east-west stretch of about two thousand square miles in southwestern South Dakota, created not by man or wind but by cloudburst waterwear and water seeping into the porous rocks, washing, washing them, remoulding their patterns and shapes, this outlandish landscape is freakish, sense-tricking, a terrible sight and grand. Out of poorly cemented bedrock there have been created spires and columns and peaks standing together and apart. There are humpbacked ridges and flat-topped buttes separated by box canyons; deep, barren gullies and sawtooth divides. On the grassy tablelands and in the low areas of this region there is scant plant and animal life. In winter devil-blizzards send their fury through this desolation. In kinder weather months it shows its colours – green, purple, gold-white. The coyotes howl at night in the awful raw stillness.

Vera and Bill Cleaver

In *Littabelle Lee,* the old unspoiled hills, the hollows and watered valleys of the Ozark mountain country are just as much a vital part of the book.

In these landscapes a sense of the presence of God is strong, and indeed the rural communities in which the Cleavers' novels are set are communities reared on God's word. But religion is in the air, in the common culture, a felt religion rather than a thought one; and attitudes can be permeated by a down-to-earth cynicism that is not the same as doubt. In the passage quoted at the beginning of this essay Mary Call Luther's trust in God is accompanied, typically, by a shrewd scepticism about what God will actually do for her; it is not the kind of trust that excuses one from keeping one's powder dry. Grover, after his mother's death, has some pertinent questions to put to the Reverend Vance, and the answers do not satisfy him – though of course the shortcoming may be that of the Reverend Vance rather than of the Christian religion. The novels are not concerned with religious inquiry or speculation, and offer no conclusions on the subject; religion, however, is there in people's backgrounds and cannot be ignored. It is intriguing that in the very first sentence of the first book Ellen Grae proclaims herself a Pantheist, but this is pure Ellen; a Pantheist is just what she *would* be. A curious sidelight is cast in *Delpha Green and Company.* Delpha's ex-convict father is now the Reverend Green, minister of his own one-man Church of Blessed Hope; Delpha herself has taken up astrology and thinks it helps her to help people solve their problems. Father's church and Delpha's astrology may well be phoney, but nevertheless Father and Delpha between them bring the people of a half-dead small town to life. It could be that what is phoney and what is genuine is to be judged by results.

A systematic appraisal of the twelve books would obviously take far more space than is available here. To me it seems that the Cleavers have not yet written a better one than *Where the Lilies Bloom,* a singularly beautiful and moving novel. Their first book for children, *Ellen Grae* – serious, funny, perceptive, splendidly crafted and holding a great deal within its few pages

– is just as remarkable in its different way, but does not give quite the same sense of dealing with universal emotional experience. *Grover, Me Too* and *The Whys and Wherefores of Littabelle Lee* show the Cleavers in their most challenging vein; they are rewarding, and even in the end enjoyable, but the enjoyment is bought at a cost of some pain. They are not light reading, and it is possible to feel that *Littabelle Lee* in particular piles on the agony too heavily. The remaining books I find slighter or less successful, though I would be sorry not to have met Ussy Mock in *The Mock Revolt* or Annie Jelks and her bright mild illegitimate nephew Calvin in *I Would Rather be a Turnip*.

By and large it is a poor, rural and curiously innocent America that emerges from the novels of Vera and Bill Cleaver. Life is hard, and must be faced with determination and without illusion. Subsistence has to be worked for. Values are traditional, good people are upright and self-respecting and inclined to be stern. The Bible is known, religion is not an embarrassment or a discarded superstition, people are conscious of God, though whether He is in their hearts or in the landscape or 'out there' somewhere is not determined, and does not need to be. Though the action takes place in the present, the past is all around it, and sometimes one feels oneself to be reading about a surviving pocket of the past. 'Endurance' is a key word. Such strenuous – indeed, pioneering – virtues are surely still to be admired and still relevant; not least in the early stages of life, which, whatever technology may do for us, remains and must always remain a long uncertain journey to the West.

Vera and Bill Cleaver

One of the Cleavers writes:

Ideally the writer of fiction comes to the task of doing so with an understanding of what fiction is. For me it is not so much the said but the unsaid. It is that which holds incident and character together, the questing voices that whisper, 'What is it? Why is it? Where are we going? What's on the other side?'

The question of why I write is put to me often but in all my years at this art or craft or madness or whatever it is I have not yet been able to translate the why of it into a distinct description. I can suppose that it is an inherent energy that pushes me toward some kind of self-validation. I say 'inherent' because I believe that only the mechanics of creative writing may be taught. As a very young child I knew that I was going to be a writer. Also, in that way children know things without being told or shown, I knew that I was going to have to be my own teacher. I have been my own teacher. I am a graduate of the public libraries of the United States of America.

I like the peace of my daily performance of brooding and poring and study and I revel in the attempts to set to page that which goes beyond the presentation of mere human behaviour. All of this digging and pushing and grinding and examination is not a bid for immortality. It is to put to work that which was given me to use for a while.

I have written of the Ozark mountaineer, of the South Dakotan, the Floridian, the rural Appalachian dweller, and so again and yet again there comes this:

Question: Do you write for any deliberately chosen audience?

Answer: No. I write of what I know. My audience is volunteer.

Question: Do you feel the need to explain the elements of your settings?

Answer: No. The explanations flow, or they should, from the philosophies in the work, from its intellectual meaning, from invested detail. If explanations are needed then, in my opinion, the work is either weak or has failed.

A Sounding of Storytellers

Question: Is the backdrop scenery in your work incidental?

Answer: Of course not. Months before I start a work I begin to gather my research material. It is requisite absolute that I know the speech of my fictional companions, know their lore. I must see their geography.

Question: Readers readily identify with stereotypes. Why do you avoid using them?

Answer: I have never seen a stereotyped situation or person. For me there resides, even in the most common, the unusual, and I want to know what it is and then through the selection of word and event tackle a demonstration.

Question: As a team how do you work together?

Answer: Well, let me tell you a little story. We have a close friend with whom we lunch several times a month. He tells us that he has trouble recognizing us when we are not together. He is serious. We have been married that long. We are joint and so all of our endeavours and opinions are joint. This is not a hedge, you understand. That is simply the way it is.

Peter Dickinson

Peter Dickinson was born in Zambia in 1927 and was educated at Eton College and King's College, Cambridge. He was the assistant editor of Punch from 1952 to 1969, and is the author of several crime novels for adults, two of which have won the Crime Writers' Association Golden Dagger Award. His children's books include The Weathermonger *(1968),* The Dancing Bear *(1972),* The Gift *(1973),* The Blue Hawk *(1976), which received the* Guardian *Award and* Chance, Luck and Destiny *(1975), which won the* Boston Globe-Horn Book *Award in 1977. Peter Dickinson is married, has four children, and lives in London.*

Peter Dickinson published little outside the pages of *Punch* until the appearance of his first novel when he was thirty-nine. In the next ten years he was to produce a score of books, alternating children's fiction with crime novels and winning awards for both.

The books for children have been extremely varied in setting and action. Some could be called, in his own phrase, 'science fiction without the science'; some are fantasy in realistic contemporary settings (or realistic fiction coloured by fantasy, depending on which way you look at it); and there is one full-blooded historical novel, set in sixth-century Byzantium and barbarian lands to the north of it, in which, however, the author admits that he 'had to invent quite a lot'. For all their variety, the books have had much in common: strong professional storytelling, rapid action and adventure, continual invention, a proliferating interest in ideas, and an understanding of how things are done. Behind all this one glimpses an energetic, speculative mind with a leaning towards the exotic. There is no great inwardness in the books, no exploration of character in

41

depth, and one feels that moral problems are touched on lightly as interesting puzzles rather than felt as taxing human dilemmas. Dickinson does not give the impression of wishing he were Tolstoy; rather, he seems to work within well-understood limits. Within these limits he has written one outstandingly fine novel, *The Blue Hawk* (1976), and at least two very good ones, *Heartsease* (1969) and *The Dancing Bear* (1972).

His first three books for children were about a time, stated to be 'now or soon', when people in Britain are supposed to have turned against machines and retreated into a new Dark Age of malicious ignorance, superstition and xenophobia: the period of the Changes. The order of the books as originally written was back-to-front. The first, *The Weathermonger* (1968), tells how the time of the Changes ended; the second, *Heartsease,* is set in the middle of the five-year period; the third, *The Devil's Children* (1970), is about the beginning. The three have since appeared the other way round in an omnibus volume, *The Changes*. It is only the situation that links them; they do not have any characters in common.

Though *The Weathermonger* and *Heartsease* were published within a year of each other, there is a striking qualitative difference between them. I cannot think of another case of comparably rapid improvement. *The Weathermonger* bears many of the marks of the first-book-for-children. The main characters, a brother and sister called Geoffrey and Sally, are a resourceful boy and girl with little in their personalities to distinguish them from other children in fiction. Conveniently there are no parents or relatives around. And the mission on which they are sent is one which, outside fiction, one cannot imagine being entrusted to children. Having got a motorboat working, and escaped in it from benighted England, they arrive at a small port in Brittany and instantly meet a French general – France is unaffected by the Changes – who dispatches them to look for the source of the trouble, rumoured to be somewhere on the Welsh borders. 'You will find out the location, the exact location of the disturbance, and then we will send missiles across. We will cauterize the disease.' The children return to England on board a ketch belonging to 'an angry millionaire, who hadn't been willing to lend it until he received a personal telephone call from the President of France'. Fortunately no missiles are needed, because Geoffrey and Sally, in the time-honoured way of fictional children, deal with the entire situation unaided.

And the explanation of the Changes is outrageous. It transpires that a Mr Furbelow, who used to keep a chemist's shop in Abergavenny, has found the sleeping body of Merlin, the wizard of Arthurian legend, and has bound Merlin to himself by getting him hooked on morphine. The powers of the revived but drug-sick magician have radiated outward and affected the population.

'I suppose,' said Geoffrey, 'it was the drugs which made him change England back to the Dark Ages. He was muddled, and wanted everything to be just as he was used to it. So he made everyone think machines were wicked, and forget how to work them.'

Merlin now lies sick in his underground chamber, but the children persuade him to renounce the drug, and after suffering withdrawal symptoms which have fearful effects on his surroundings Merlin returns to his long rest and normality is restored. This is, to my mind, an abuse of major legend, as well as being totally unconvincing.

Yet *The Weathermonger* has some very good things in it. There is a splendid dash across a hostile England in a 1900 Rolls Royce Silver Ghost from the Montague Motor Museum at Beaulieu. And although it is not clear why an effect of the Changes should have been to give a few people the power of making the weather they want, the author himself makes brilliantly effective use of this notion. Geoffrey happens to be a weathermonger – hence the title – and the passages in which he conjures weather-changes are at once poetic and meteorologically precise.

He felt for the clouds with his mind. From above they were silver, and the sun trampled on them, ramming his gold heels uselessly into their clotting softness. But there were frail places in the fabric. Push now, sun, here, at this weakness, ram through with a gold column, warming the under air, hammering it hard, as a smith hammers silver. Turn now, air, in a slow spiral, widening, a spring of summer, warmth drawing in more air as the thermal rises to push the clouds apart, letting in more sun to warm the under-air. Now the fields steam, and in the clouds there is a turning lake of blue, a turning sea, spinning the rain away. More sun. . .

On its first appearance, *The Weathermonger,* in my view, was praised beyond its true deserts; yet its reception does credit to the reviewers, whose most important task is to recognize new talent, and who certainly did so in this case.

In the other two books of the sequence no more is said about the cause of the Changes. It is simply assumed that they have happened; and, given that assumption, everything else follows. There is no further fantasy element. In *Heartsease,* Margaret and her cousin Jonathan, who are both fourteen and live on a farm, find a 'witch' – actually an American investigator who has been stoned and left for dead. They and Lucy, the house servant, look after him, take him by sledge through a snow-covered countryside to Gloucester docks, hide him on a tug, and later run the gauntlet of the ship-canal to get him safely to sea. In *The Devil's Children* Nicola, aged twelve, is adopted by a group of Sikhs, who are unaffected by the Changes but endangered by the attitudes that result from them, and helps the Sikhs to set up a successful rural community in the face of local hostility. *Heartsease* in particular is a well-shaped, well-told story, with unified action and interest. Jonathan, who knows about engines, and Margaret, who knows about horses, are a complementary pair and make a good team; and though the servant girl Lucy does not play a big part, there is an intriguing sense that there's a good deal more to Lucy than might appear on the surface. Dickinson has described *Heartsease* as 'a winter book, harsh and claustrophobic';[1] but there is warmth in its human relation-

1. Peter Dickinson, 'Author of Today', *Books for Your Children,* February 1971.

ships, and it ends with Margaret riding home on her horse Scrub, on a morning when 'weald and wold were singing with early spring' and 'every breath she took was full of the odour of new growth, a smell as strong as hyacinths'. *The Devil's Children,* though not I think quite so good a novel as *Heartsease,* has a fine robust climax in which the Sikhs live up to their martial reputation and defeat a band of robbers in pitched battle.

A curious feature of these three books is their assumption that ignorance and malice go hand in hand with the rejection of machinery. It is not unreasonable to suppose this, and it is certainly useful for the author's fictional purposes; but it is not a self-evident proposition, except perhaps to those who unthinkingly equate 'modern' with 'good'. Peter Dickinson himself is not one of these. *The Weathermonger* ends with the rueful observation that 'the English air would soon be reeking with petrol'; and in *Heartsease* there is a moment when Margaret says that 'they're right about machines, somehow . . . Machines eat your mind up until you think they're the answer to everything.' But these are isolated remarks: very little to set in the balance against an overwhelming general sense that 'our' side is the side of the machines. As in some other places in his work, Peter Dickinson is aware of an issue and makes his awareness clear, but backs away from any serious dealings with it.

Another three Dickinson books, though without formal links, can conveniently be looked at together. These are the ones that have contemporary settings but also fantasy elements. In *Emma Tupper's Diary* (1971), the young McAndrew cousins with whom fourteen-year-old Emma is staying decide to reactivate the miniature submarine which Grandfather built many years ago, and use it in the loch beside which they live, to hoodwink a television company by simulating a monster. And then Emma and cousin Roddy, submarining unofficially at night, find that truth can be stranger than hoaxes.

The social background here is somewhat aristocratic. The McAndrews live on their own land, surrounded by retainers and clansfolk, and Father is the clan chief: he has 'never had a job, except during wars', but 'he's been everywhere and seen everything and met everyone . . . and whenever an Honours List is published he has to spend several days writing to all his cronies who've become Lords and things'. His son Andy dazzles girls with his 'looks and money and style'. It seems almost indecent in these days when children's books are expected by many to reflect the lives of ordinary people rather than the privileged; but in fact the participants and setting are right for the story, and there is no obvious reason why any social class should be excluded from the literary scene. There is a strong contrast, however, between the McAndrews and the family of Davy Price in *The Gift* (1973). The Prices are much more humble folk: the grandparents on their Welsh hill farm, Mum and Dad in the little house in the new town. Davy's gift, passed down in the family for generations, is that of seeing the pictures formed in other people's minds. It seems to him fairly harmless, though a bit of a nuisance, until the day he finds himself looking into the violent, destructive mentality of a dangerous psychopath. A sequence of events then leads to a situation in which only Davy, still using his gift, can avert a mass slaughter.

At one point in *Annerton Pit* (1977), Dickinson's latest book for children at the time of writing, there is a similar phenomenon to that of Davy's gift. Blind boy Jake and older brother Martin, looking for their missing grandfather, have stumbled on the Green Revolutionaries (militant environmentalists), who are using an abandoned mine on the Northumbrian coast as headquarters for an attempt to hijack a North Sea oil-rig. When all three are imprisoned in the old workings, it is Jake – his blindness no longer a disadvantage – who leads the way out. But in the course of the escape Jake, while alone, encounters a being which appears to inhabit the hill, to feel the workings as a wound, and to defend itself by communicating terror. Jake appears to perceive what the thing perceives and feel as it feels; but the possibility is left open that it exists only in his own mind. And yet at the end, when one of the Green Revolutionary activists blows up the workings, 'Dyingly, the air moved up the shaft as the last compression of the explosion eased itself out of

the maze of galleries below. To Jake it sounded like a whispering sigh of content.'

Of these three books, all with contemporary settings yet with
touches of the exotic, *Emma Tupper* is the most satisfying. In
most ways it is the simplest. It is a variation on the old holiday
adventure story: an unusually good one, with a strong
storyline, tense moments, a splendid surprise, and a good deal
of high-spirited humour and wordplay. The descriptions of the
launching and operation of the miniature submarine are a fascinating technical *tour de force*. Emma's diary is deftly handled in
such a way as to escape the improbabilities inherent in this kind
of first-person narration: namely, an undue literary sophistica-
tion and a length so inordinate that the diarist would have had
no time for the activities described. Here the diary is merely
referred to in italic opening paragraphs at the heads of chapters;
and the few words quoted from it are perfectly credible as the
work of a fourteen-year-old. The author's way of dealing with
the problem set by the discovery of a colony of real-life monsters – a species of plesiosaur – in a cave beneath the loch surface
is particularly ingenious. Should the discovery be exploited, or
made available only to scientists, or kept secret? The argument
is organized in the shape of a family conference, with appeals on
points of order, requests to address remarks to the chair, casting
votes and the other apparatus of meetings. The result is to
dramatize the matter, express character through it, incorporate
it into the body of the fiction – and incidentally to demonstrate
that discussion of an issue can be included in a children's novel
without loss of impetus.

The Gift is less successful. Perhaps it tries to work on two
planes at once and doesn't quite succeed on either. At one level,
the author has had material for an effective thriller, but he has
not been content to write a thriller. His criminal is no mere
baddie but is mentally ill, a pathetic creature. Davy's family
background is drawn in much more detail than would be
needed for an action story alone – an important part of the
matter of the book is the situation of Davy and sister Penny in a
home where Dad is always likely to mess things up and Mum

might skip off at any time – yet although in plot terms the family problems, the crime theme and Davy's gift are linked together, they do not cohere emotionally. And the effect of the gift on Davy himself is surely underplayed.

Annerton Pit also seems to try to do too much, and raises more issues than it deals with. The morality of violence, when used to advance a cause, is touched on but not seriously examined; the psychological roots of violence likewise. And the mine, or maze, with a monster in it has symbolic and mythological associations of which the author is certainly well aware. But all these strands are thin and wispy, not woven into a fabric. *Annerton Pit* can of course, and by a great many young readers will, be read as a straight adventure story, and it's quite a good one: the escape through the workings of the pit achieves a prolonged and well-sustained tension. Even in this aspect however, as in others, Dickinson's two remaining books, *The Dancing Bear* and *The Blue Hawk,* are stronger and stranger.

The Dancing Bear tells of the sack of a great house in Byzantium, and the journey into Hunnish lands of Silvester, a slave, in search of the abducted daughter of the house. He is accompanied by Holy John, a dirty old domestic saint with a new-found mission to convert the barbarians, and Bubba, the bear of whom Silvester is keeper. It is a vigorous, rich and close-textured story; episodic, as quest stories must be, but fully controlled and shaped. There is always something going on: the book is alive with colourful and humorous incident. On a trip to the quayside at Byzantium, early in the story, for instance:

Silvester found the two porters in the Tavern of the Holy Toe, drunk but not so drunk that they couldn't point out the two beggars they'd hired to stay sober for them. One of these beggars was at least seventy, and the other had lost a leg and walked with a crutch. Because of his throat, Luke [the cook, who has come to the harbour to buy fish] couldn't shout his rage, but he snatched the crutch and started to beat all four men with it. The old man ran away, but the drunks and the cripple skipped and yelled until one of the harbour policemen strolled across and told Luke to stop unless he had evidence that the men were heretics.

A contrast between civilized and barbarian life runs all through the book. Holy John points out to Silvester near the end of the journey that he has travelled from 'a city of intricate beauties and also of intricate evils' to 'a land of simple beauties and of simple evils'. And Silvester encounters – later to serve and to succeed – the Slav Antoninus, who has established an outpost of order and tradition in a lost imperial province, proclaimed himself Roman, and 'lived his lie until it became true'. Silvester himself belongs to civilization and moreover is a slave, knowing his place and knowing his value 'almost to a coin'. Though intelligent and able, he expects to be told what to do by his superiors, and only when the rescued Lady Ariadne gives him his manumission can he approach her as man to woman. He marries her, but for him at least it is only a modified happy ending, because he is exiled from the empire: he will never again cross the Danube, never return to the Byzantium he has loved. Holy John, combative and intensely opinionated, throws a shrewd oblique light on the nature of sainthood. And Bubba – stupid, affectionate, soppy, irritable – is a triumph of animal characterization; she is presented with a humorous half-anthropomorphism that never contradicts her animal nature or sinks to facetiousness.

Peter Dickinson's brief foreword to *The Dancing Bear* is illuminating. After summarizing the state of affairs in city and empire in 558 A.D., he goes on: 'And still the tides of savage nations flood out of Russia, for gold and cattle and the glory of slaughter.' The choice of words should be noted: tides, savage, flood, gold, cattle, glory, slaughter. They are powerful and evocative, a storyteller's words rather than an academic historian's, and in their context none the worse for that. *The Dancing Bear* is a splendid piece of storytelling.

Nevertheless, *The Blue Hawk* is Peter Dickinson's most impressive novel up to the time of writing. Set in a land that suggests ancient Egypt, at a time that is remote and perhaps hypothetical rather than past or future, it tells of a boy priest Tron, servant of Gdu, the god of hawking and healing. The god speaks in Tron's heart, bids him save a hawk from sacrifice and break a ritual; this causes the death of a king and sets moving a train of events that are to open up a closed land and free powers that have been rigidly bound. There is no lack of the continuous action which characterizes a Dickinson novel. But this is only part of the story. *The Blue Hawk* is about a struggle for power in a closely-controlled, priest-ridden society where everything that happens is governed by ritual, knowledge is transmitted by memorized hymns and nothing can change; yet without change the fields will silt up with salt and the land will die of inanition if it is not killed by savage enemies.

Behind the political struggle lies a further question: do the gods exist, other than as a source of power for priests? One might think not; myth and management are the same thing in this rigid society. Yet Tron *experiences* the presence of the gods; it was a god's speaking to him that set moving the wave of change. Perhaps he is indeed the instrument of higher powers, perhaps what happens had to happen. At the end Tron offers his own explanation, though only 'as a story'. The gods, he suggests, do exist but don't belong in this world; they are immensely powerful but not clever and have been trapped by wise men (as it might be ourselves). Maybe they have wanted to break out and away, and a great ritual in which Tron took part near the end of the book has opened the way for them to go. Yet this may be 'just guesses'; or may be an image for something of which we are unable to grasp the truth. And yet again, when Tron is asked whether he thinks the gods have flown and there are none any more, he says that there must be:

'I've got something in my soul which is there to love and serve the gods. So even if all my supposings are right there must still be the true gods of this world to love and serve. . . Perhaps the true gods are . . . inside us, all round us, like the air we breathe without noticing. The noise these other gods made meant we could never hear them.'

There is no need to go further into these perplexities. The author is not laying it on the line, declaring in unambiguous terms what is going on. Tron does not know what the gods are;

he can only wait, be ready, be receptive. Within his imaginative framework, Dickinson has left room for the imagination of the reader to move; and the reader, too, can speculate – if he wishes to do so. Alternatively he can just read the story. There is plenty to make him want to turn the page.

There is a great deal of violence in *The Blue Hawk,* with nothing spared: at one point a grisly cairn of priests' heads; at another, mothers hurling their children over a cliff to destruction on the rocks below, before leaping to their own deaths. Dickinson has said he thinks the style of writing and the context make these horrors acceptably distant from the young reader's world,[2] and this comment would presumably also apply to various violent incidents in the other books. There are moments, however, when violence is seen closer up and in a different light, with the apparent implication that it is something to be accepted. Tron watches his hawk make a kill, and

it struck him for the first time how strange it was that the perfection of the moment had to end in a death. It was as though he were a god who needed the sacrifice of the kingfowl to fulfil his nature. Were the gods indeed like that? No. It was the blue hawk that needed the death, to fulfil *its* nature.

Closer to ourselves, one recalls that Nicky in *The Devil's Children* felt a kinship with the robber who 'laughed like a lover' as he swung his axe; one recalls, too, Jake's reflection at the end of *Annerton Pit* that 'if you mine down through the maze of your own being, perhaps in those deeps you will find the explosive gas of violence, the springs of love'.

These last aspects of violence – questions of the necessity of it, the attraction of it, its association with fulfilment and even with love – are the most difficult and worrying ones in the Dickinson novels. The psychology of violence can be explored in adult fiction but is probably too complex, too demanding in terms of experience and understanding required from the reader, and

2. Interview with Peter Dickinson by Lesley Adamson, *Guardian*, 31 March 1977.

perhaps too disturbing, to be dealt with in depth in novels for children. In spite of the reference to 'mining down through the maze of your own being', Peter Dickinson does not, I think, attempt such exploration; and he is probably right not to do so (though it may be questioned whether, this being so, the more intimate encounters with violence, as distinct from the 'acceptably distant' variety, might not be better omitted). This may be a point at which Dickinson, like other writers in other respects, comes up against the boundaries of the children's list. Or it may be that he comes up against a personal boundary: that he does not go deeply down into the human heart because that is not the kind of writer he is. The latter hypothesis, if correct, is not a cause for complaint. Writers must do what they can and want to do; and Peter Dickinson can do things in fiction that less fertile and vigorous contemporaries would never have the creative energy to achieve.

Peter Dickinson

Peter Dickinson writes:

I prefer not to think, let alone write, coherently about how I do what I do, or why, or even for whom. Part of the reason will be obvious to anyone who has ever had an on day at some sport, say tennis: the moment you start to wonder what you're doing right your game goes to pieces. Another part of the reason is that I might grow to the shape of my theories – one of the pleasures of writing for children is that it is a sufficiently small world for a single writer to be able to explore large districts of it.

The Stevenson of *Treasure Island* is, I suppose, my Socrates and the Kipling of *Rewards and Fairies* my Plato. But though I am aware of working inside a strong tradition I regard myself as a primitive. I have a function, like the village cobbler, and that is to tell stories. Everything else is subservient to that. This doesn't mean that everything else can be left out (though I do know books which are abysmally written, for instance, and yet tell their story well enough to be good books). For example, if a story needs a priestly caste, those priests have to have gods to worship, and a coherent theology, and besides that they must come from a society in which it makes sense to devote a proportion of the men to the priesthood, and an economy that will support the extra mouths, and so on. These needn't be endlessly described, but I must have imagined them as I wrote so that the reader can be subliminally aware of them as he reads. The same applies to vaguer concepts, even to what is normally called the 'idea' of a book. For me, it is there because the story is there, and not the other way round.

If I fight shy of positive notions about my writing, I do have one fairly coherent negative belief. It's about what I'm not doing. I am not whittling rungs for the great ladder that leads up to Lawrence and Proust. I think children read differently from adults, and have a different use for books. (I also think that many adults have never learnt to read the way adults are supposed to, which accounts in part for the decline of the novel.) To me the great ladder tradition is something of a tyranny. So if, for instance, the intricate development and exploration of character plays no great part in my stories, that's because I don't think it is a proper element in the genre. People have to have characters, of course, in the same way that priests have to have theologies; but if I get it right then the person is there in the book, clear and rounded-seeming, and the reader acknowledges her existence and gets on with the story.

Finally, I am strongly against the religion of art, and the priesthood of artists. I am a cobbler. Given good leather I can make a comfortable shoe.

Paula Fox

Paula Fox was born in New York City. Her mother was Spanish, her father a writer, Paul Harvey Fox. She has two sons and lives in Brooklyn with her husband, who is a professor. She has written short stories, television plays and adult novels in addition to her books for children, which include How Many Miles to Babylon? *(1967),* The Stone-Faced Boy *(1968),* Blowfish Live in the Sea *(1970) and* The Slave Dancer *(1973), for which she was awarded the Newbery Medal.*

Of the new writers for children who emerged in the United States in the later 1960s, Paula Fox was quickly seen to be one of the most able. Her books were unusually varied; each had a distinct individual character, but at the same time each was stamped with her own imprint. And they had an air of newness: not merely the literal contemporaneity which almost anyone can achieve but the newness that comes from looking at things with new eyes, feeling them in a new way.

In the 1950s and early 1960s, a traditional and generally reassuring view of children and their role had run through the work of the leading and well-established children's writers. Childhood was part of a continuing pattern – the orderly succession of the generations – and children were growing up to take their place in a known and understood world. As the 1960s went on, it was perceived increasingly that this pattern did not reflect reality. Families and societies were not stable; the older generation was not regarded, and did not even regard itself, as the repository of all wisdom, and it could not be assumed that young people were anxious to grow up and join it. The generation gap had opened up, and before long writers for young people were trooping into it, often in a worried, heavy-footed and anxious-to-be-with-it way.

Paula Fox was one of the small number of writers who brought quick sharp perceptions to the new and in many ways uneasy scene, and also an instinctive sympathy for the young who (just as much as their parents) had to deal with it. A recurrent theme in her work of the late 1960s, and again in *Blowfish Live in the Sea* (1970), is that of non-communication and lack of understanding between young and old. But she is not a writer who could be content to mine a single narrow seam. She has written both adult and young people's novels; she has produced picture books and younger children's stories; and her most substantial work on the children's lists up to the time of writing, the award-winning *The Slave Dancer* (1973), is a historical novel of weight and intensity which stands on its own, at a distance from her other books.

Her early books for children have central characters aged from about eight to ten, but one would hesitate to say that they are 'for' readers of such an age. The audience and the author's position in relation to it seem curiously fluid. One has no sense that the writer, as an adult, is *here,* in charge, handing it out, while the audience of children is *there*, duly taking it. If there is a message in the air, it is probably for someone quite different. The first two, *Maurice's Room* (1966) and *A Likely Place* (1967), are not telling children anything except a story, but seem rather obviously to be saying something to parents: don't fuss the child, let him grow in his own way. The two books are humorous, even witty, but in a way that one would expect to appeal to readers rather older than their heroes. And the third and best of the early books, *How Many Miles to Babylon?* (1967), whose hero is barely ten, was one of only two books specifically recommended for teenagers by Nat Hentoff in the *Atlantic* for December 1967. The conventional wisdom is that children and teenagers don't want to read about children younger than themselves, and this generally appears to be true. But it could be that discussion of the question betrays a more fixed attitude than Paula Fox would adopt. Who says who is to read what?

Like many other writers, she raises the question 'For whom?', and as with many other writers I can find no answer except 'For whom it may concern.'

Maurice's Room is in fact a blessedly funny book; and as for readership, one can only try it on and see if the glove fits. Maurice at eight is dedicated to his collection of junk, which spills over everything. His parents feel he needs more constructive interests, and often discuss him with their friends.

Some visitors said that collections like Maurice's showed that a child would become a great scientist. Many great scientists had collected junk when they were eight years old. Other visitors said Maurice would outgrow his collection and become interested in other things, such as money or armies. Some suggested to the Henrys that they ought to buy Maurice a dog, or send him to music school so that his time might be spent more usefully.

And his parents, with the best intentions, get everything wrong. The dog they borrow to be a companion to Maurice is in fact a dreadful nuisance to him, yet Mother is soon convinced that 'Maurice and Patsy are inseparable.' An attempt to get Maurice to learn an instrument is disastrous. The beautiful sailboat that Mr Henry buys Maurice for his birthday is forgotten while Maurice and friend grope for some old bedsprings lying on the bottom of the pond. 'If I had known you wanted bedsprings instead of a beautiful three-foot sailing ketch, I would have gotten you bedsprings,' says poor Mr Henry in despair. Finally, Maurice's parents decide to move to the country, where they hope that everything will be different. And this time at least all is well, for although Maurice isn't terribly interested in the country as such, there is an old barn that already holds the nucleus of a promising new junk collection. It's a hilarious, subversive book, full of casual joys. One can see that Maurice will survive the well-meant but uncomprehending intrusions of adults, just as will Lewis in *A Likely Place*. Lewis, too, is fussed by the grown-ups, but is fortunately left by his parents in the charge of eccentric Miss Fitchlow, who goes in for yogurt and yoga, calls Lewis 'pal', and lets him off the lead.

Which is just what he needed. It is a short, dry, subtle book; and if there is a lesson in it, then I suspect that, as in *Maurice's Room,* it is really a lesson for parents.

Paula Fox's third book, *How Many Miles to Babylon?*, is a longer novel of much greater depth and complexity. Its hero, James, is a small black boy living in Brooklyn, whose father has disappeared and whose mother has gone into hospital, leaving him in the care of three elderly aunts. One day he walks out of school and goes to play by himself in an empty house. In his mind is a story that his mother has really gone to her own country across the seas and that he is secretly a prince. Three small boys, not much older than James but tougher, capture him and make him help them work their dog-stealing racket. James travels frightening miles with them on the back of a bicycle, goes to a deserted funhouse on Coney Island, sees the Atlantic. At night he frees the stolen dogs, runs away, gets home to the old aunts, and finds his mother there. She is back from hospital; she is no princess and he no prince. 'Hello, Jimmy,' she says.

On the surface it is a straightforward story, with its strong plot about the fearful boy and the tough gang and the dogs and the juvenile racketeering. But there are strange undertones: the symbolic voyage, the 'other' story of James which is only hinted at. The action, although shadows are cast before and behind it in time, takes place within a day and a night. 'Can I get there by candlelight? Yes, and back again.' Both action and setting are almost dreamlike; the landscape an intimately-known landscape yet glimpsed as if in shifting mists. Everything is experienced through James; and James himself is wandering in a mist of illusion, though eventually compelled by what happens to grasp at rough reality. It is felt in every page, but never said in crude terms, that James is a member of a submerged race and class, and isolated even within that. He is not a sharply-drawn character, nor meant to be, for the reader will suffer with him rather than observe him from the outside; but the minor characters – the three old aunts, the three young rack-eteers – are clear in outline, defined by the words they speak.

Paula Fox

In one sense the outcome of *How Many Miles to Babylon?* is plain. James has proved himself, has faced the actual world, found and accepted his actual mother. He has come through. But to say that is not enough. Illusion and reality, the symbolic and the actual, are not to be so neatly separated. There is much in the book that the mind cannot simply deal with and eject. The inner mystery is something to be carried about and wondered at from time to time rather than be resolved.

The same might be said of *The Stone-Faced Boy* (1968), whose hero Gus – the middle child of five, about ten years old, timid, vulnerable, shut-off – goes out into the snow at night to free a stray dog from a trap. Gus, too, proves himself; finds the key that will help him to overcome his problems. But again this is not quite all. *The Stone-Faced Boy* is a winter's tale, with the quiet, real-yet-unreal feeling of a white landscape. There is a shiver in it, too: a ghostliness. The trap in which the dog is caught belongs to an old man, who takes Gus home to his cottage, full of the debris of the past, for a cup of tea with his equally old wife. And at one point the old man tells the old lady to show Gus how spry she is.

> She made a strange little jump and then, holding her skirt out with her two hands, she did a little dance in front of the stove, smiling, wobbling slightly, kicking one foot out, then the other. Then she fell back softly into the rocker, like a feather coming to rest.

On the previous page we have heard that the old lady 'had a light, free laugh, and to Gus's surprise the sound reminded him of Serena'. Serena is his younger sister, aged about eight: nice, dreamy, imaginative. Gus feels it is impossible for Serena to get so old. But of course she will; this delicate tying together of the two ends of life makes one of the book's many quiet yet admirable achievements.

Portrait of Ivan (1969) does not have the mysterious depths of *How Many Miles to Babylon?* or *The Stone-Faced Boy,* but has subtleties and satisfactions of its own. It is a brief novel about a boy of eleven who leads a dull, lonely life, walled in by well-to-do, conventional, adult-dominated surroundings. The walls about him begin to crack when he meets the painter Matt and the elderly reader-aloud Miss Manderby, and start collapsing rapidly as he potters about in a boat with a barefoot girl called Geneva. There is a key sentence to the understanding of one aspect of Paula Fox when Ivan realizes that in his life in the city

he was nearly always being taken to or from some place by an adult, in nearly every moment of his day he was holding on to a rope held at the other end by a grown-up person – a teacher or a bus driver, a housekeeper or a relative. But since he had met Matt, space had been growing all around him. It was frightening to let go of that rope, but it made him feel light and quick instead of heavy and slow.

Ivan has needed space in which to open out, yet by a near-paradox, in order to open out he needs a framework, a context for his own life, a sense of who and what he is and how he got here. He has been living in what might be called a cramped void. It is something important when his friend draws for him the imagined sledge on which his mother, whom he never knew, left Russia as a child, a little girl who 'did not know she had begun a journey that led right to this room where her son now lay, half asleep'. That is a link that Ivan needed.

Ben, in *Blowfish Live in the Sea,* is eighteen and although the book is largely about him, the viewpoint is that of his half-sister Carrie, aged twelve. Though Ben is older than Ivan, his emotional position is somewhat similar, in that, just as Ivan needed the link with his mother in order to orientate himself, Ben needs to find his father. But Ben's father is not dead; he is a drifter, a pathetic, unsatisfactory person. Ben's mother has divorced and remarried, and Ben has a stable, prosperous home, but he is totally alienated. He has dropped out of school, got rid of all his possessions, and Carrie sees him as

a tall thin person in a droopy coat with the collar up. The person's hands are shoved into the coat pockets; the threads that stick out from the places where buttons used to be are a different color from the cloth of the coat. When he walks, the person looks down at his feet as they move forward in cracked muddy boots.

Paula Fox

'Blowfish live in the sea' is the message that Ben writes on brown paper bags, on unopened letters, in dust on window-panes; and the explanation is that his father once sent him a blowfish – round as a soccer ball, stiff with varnish, orange and yellow and shiny – with a letter describing it as a souvenir from the upper reaches of the Amazon. Ben's graffito is a comment on this shabby deception. But when his father turns up, a perennial failure with nothing to his name but a seedy rundown motel, Ben decides to join him: 'He needs some help to get it into shape. He doesn't have hardly any money. . . . The place is a wreck.' We leave Ben starting on the carpentry, keeping his father off the drink; we don't know how long it will last, but we know it is something positive for Ben at last and will be the making of him.

This is the principal strand of the book, but there are others. Running through it all is Carrie's affection for Ben. As she looks at him, dusty and sad, with the rawhide thong round the hair that he won't get cut, Carrie remarks, 'Sometimes I thought I loved him better than anyone.' And in his desultory way Ben returns the affection; in fact there are traces everywhere of a loving, more open Ben. Although Ben belongs strictly to his time, and although people of his age already look different and behave differently, he is not in the least invalidated as a character by subsequent change. The underlying human nature can be seen quite clearly within the pattern formed by its interaction with outward circumstances.

Paula Fox is obviously much concerned with relationships between children and adults. She is conscious that in a compli-cated and rapidly changing society it is hard for the generations to live together satisfactorily. It will not do for grown-ups to think in terms of feeding a child into the production line and in due course drawing off an adult from the other end; but neither can young people really write off the older generation, ignoring it as irrelevant or hating it as the enemy.

Her books for younger children are a mixed collection, and in my view have not always been successful. They include a curious, way-out picture book *Hungry Fred* (1969), about a boy

61

who eats his way through the contents of a house, the house itself and the backyard, and is still hungry. Then he makes friends with a wild rabbit as big as himself. 'The rabbit leaned against Fred. Fred smiled. He felt full.' It is difficult to see what young children will make of this. And although one accepts that a picture book, like a poem or story, does not have to be understood in literal terms in order to make its impact, there needs to be an imaginative power and unity which I do not find in *Hungry Fred,* and which the artist, understandably, could not supply. *Good Ethan* (1973), about a small boy who ingeniously solves the problem of retrieving his new ball from the wrong side of a street he has been told not to cross, is a simpler and more satisfactory conception, and benefits from pictures by Arnold Lobel which are exactly in key with it. Paula Fox is also the author of *The Little Swineherd and Other Tales* (1978); a group of short, folk-type stories set in the odd framework of an attempt by a duck – yes, a duck – to succeed in show business. The duck is promoting the actual storyteller – a goose who simply likes to tell stories – and there is dry satiric humour in the account of the duck's attempts at exploitation and his uncomprehending interventions in the creative process. But the book as a whole does not quite work. Russell Hoban would have done this kind of thing better. The title story, however, about the half-starved and neglected boy who takes over a smallholding when its owners disappear and has vastly improved it by the time they come back to reclaim their property, is a touching and memorable one; it would have been preferable, I believe, to present it on its own.

I have left until last the book which, so far, is Paula Fox's finest achievement. I do not think it could have been predicted from her earlier work that she would write such a book as *The Slave Dancer.* It is the story of Jessie Bollier, a boy who is pressed into the crew of the slave ship *Moonlight* in 1840 for a voyage to Africa, picking up a cargo of blacks to be sold in Cuba. This is a case where the discipline of writing for the children's list has been wholly to the benefit of the book as a work of art. The 'young eye at the centre' is no mere convention of the adventure story for children; it is the one perspective from which the witnessing of dreadful events can be fully and freshly experienced, and at the same time the moral burden be made clear. Jessie is horrified by the treatment of the slaves, but he is powerless to prevent it; moreover he is young, white, and one of the crew, and the oppressors are his fellow-countrymen.

Jessie plays the fife, and his job is to make music to which, for brief periods daily, the slaves can exercise. This is called dancing the slaves. The aim is to keep them (relatively) healthy and therefore marketable, in spite of the crowded and filthy conditions in which they live. A slave has no human value but has a financial one: a dead slave is a lost profit. As the voyage goes on, the slaves, crammed together in the reeking hold, become sick, half-starved and hopeless, most of them suffering from 'the bloody flux', an affliction that makes the latrine buckets inadequate. And Jessie finds that 'a dreadful thing' is happening in his mind:

I hated the slaves! I hated their shuffling, their howling, their very suffering! I hated the way they spat out their food upon the deck, the overflowing buckets, the emptying of which tried all my strength. I hated the foul stench that came from the holds no matter which way the wind blew, as though the ship itself were soaked with human excrement. I would have snatched the rope from Spark's [the mate's] hand and beaten them myself! Oh, God! I wished them all dead! Not to hear them! Not to smell them! Not to know of their existence!

The Slave Dancer is not a story solely of horror. It is also a novel of action, violence and suspense, culminating in shipwreck (which was indeed the fate of a slaver called *Moonlight* in the Gulf of Mexico in 1840; the actual names of her crew are used). Jessie and a black boy named Ras with whom he has made a precarious friendship are the only survivors; they reach land and there is a limited happy ending. Ras is set on the road to freedom; Jessie gets home to his mother and sister, is apprenticed, lives an ordinary, modestly-successful life, and fights in the Civil War on the Union side.

A Sounding of Storytellers

After the war my life went on much like my neighbors' lives. I no longer spoke of my journey on a slave ship back in 1840. I did not often think of it myself. Time softened my memory as though it was kneading wax. But there was one thing that did not yield to time.

I was unable to listen to music. I could not bear to hear a woman sing, and at the sound of any instrument, a fiddle, a flute, a drum, a comb with paper wrapped around it played by my own child, I would leave instantly and shut myself away. For at the first note of a tune or of a song, I would see once again, as though they'd never ceased their dancing in my mind, black men and women and children lifting their tormented limbs in time to a reedy martial air, the dust rising from their joyless thumping, the sound of the fife finally drowned beneath the clanging of their chains.

Those are the closing sentences of *The Slave Dancer*. Ultimately the book is not depressing; the human spirit is not defeated. But it is permeated through and through by the horror it describes. The casual brutality of the ordinary seamen towards the slaves is as fearful in its way as the more positive and corrupt cruelty of the captain and mate and the revolting, hypocritical crew member Ben Stout. For the seamen are 'not especially cruel save in their shared and unshakable conviction that the least of them was better than any black alive'. They are merely ignorant. Villainy is exceptional by definition, but dreadful things done by decent men, to people whom they manage to look on as not really human, are a reminder of our own self-deceit and lack of imagination, of the capacity we all have for evil. There, but for the grace of God, go all of us.

Is such knowledge fit for children? Yes, it is; they ought not to grow up without it. This book looks at a terrifying side of human nature, and one which – in the specific manifestation of the slave trade – has left deeply-planted obstacles in the way of human brotherhood. The implication was made plain by Paula Fox in her Newbery acceptance speech in 1974. We must face this history of evil, and our capacity for evil, if the barriers are ever to come down.

Paula Fox

Paula Fox writes:

My career sounds like flap copy of the 1930s. The strangest, but not the worst, job I ever had was punctuating Italian madrigals of the fifteenth century. I assume my employer thought my guess was as good as his. I worked in Europe for a year, for Victor Gollancz, then as a string reporter for a news agency. I've taught school for seven years, sold two television plays, written four novels for grown-ups.

I never think I'm writing for children when I work. A story does not start for anyone, nor an idea, nor a feeling of an idea; but starts more for oneself. . . I think any story is a metaphor. It is not life. There is no way out but to pick a glove that conforms most to the hand. But the glove is never the hand, only a shape. And a child's hand is not an adult's. So, of course, I do write for children, or for adults. But the connection between them, the differences even, don't seem to me to be really relevant, only talking-points. What applies to good writing is, I think, absolute, whether for children or grown-ups, or the blind or the deaf or the thin or the fat. . .

Leon Garfield

Leon Garfield was born in Brighton in 1921. He was for a time an art student before joining the Army and serving for five years of the Second World War in England, Belgium and Germany. He worked for some years as a hospital biochemist, but is now a full-time writer. His books include Devil-in-the-Fog *(1966), which won the* Guardian *Award,* Smith *(1967), winner of an Arts Council award,* The Prisoners of September *(1975) and* The Confidence Man *(1978). He received the Carnegie Medal for* The God Beneath the Sea *(1970), which he wrote in collaboration with Edward Blishen. Leon Garfield lives in Highgate, London, with his wife and daughter.*

'I have livelier expectations from Leon Garfield,' I wrote in *A Sense of Story*, 'than from anyone else whose work is being published on a children's list in England today.' That was in 1971, seven years after the appearance of Garfield's first book. He has now doubled his span as a published writer. Obviously, at the end of the second seven years, it is time to ask whether these expectations have been fulfilled. The answer surely must be that they have: he has added more, and more variously, to the body of his work than any children's writer of comparable standing.

It is true that Garfield is no longer the startling phenomenon he once was. Commentators have grown used to him, and inevitably have come to take many of his positive qualities for granted while paying more attention to his faults and limitations. New writers are exciting; established ones become part of the scenery. It happens to everyone; it has happened to Leon Garfield to the extent that, on rereading the books of his second seven years, I wonder whether they have received the attention they deserve, or have been looked on (wrongly) as 'more of the same'. The major books of this period – *The Strange Affair of Adelaide Harris* (1971), *The Ghost Downstairs* (1972), *The Sound of Coaches* (1974), *The Prisoners of September* (1975), *The Pleasure Garden* (1976) and the sequence known as *Garfield's Apprentices* (1978) – add up to a remarkable achievement. They are not necessarily more successful than the early ones; they have pushed out the author's bounds into territories that may be less fruitful in terms of appreciation by young readers; but they show Leon Garfield as a writer whose work has grown in range, in depth and in complexity.

In the earlier books, the most obvious and striking of the Garfield characteristics were already in evidence. From the beginning he treated the English language with a mastery that verged on outrage, and that has not diminished, though it has been more disciplined in later work. At no time would it have been possible to mistake a page of Garfield for a page by anyone else. His exuberant energy, his extravagant yet splendidly apt images, were accompanied by a nonstop flow of outward and visible action; the people he created were vastly larger, livelier, more vivid than life. And this mode of writing created its own probabilities. Wildly unlikely it might be, for instance, that the waif Smith should be rewarded with ten thousand guineas by the not-conspicuously-generous heirs to a fortune, but like many farther-fetched events this was entirely acceptable because nothing less would have matched the size of the story.

These earlier novels were all set in the eighteenth century and mostly in London; a combination of place and period that he has continued to favour, although by now he has several times moved outside it. The choice of the eighteenth century is an unexplained mystery of the Garfield writing personality. It could be that it allows release from the realistic inhibitions that increasingly gathered round the novel from mid-Victorian times onwards. Garfield's is a lawless world; or, more precisely, a world in which the rule of law is itself a contender, is trying to assert itself but is not to be relied on for protection. People are dependent on their own quickness of hand, of foot, of eye, of wit. The world is one in which great and small rogues are forever busy and the Devil is there to take the hindmost. When writing of this time, the author appears to be steeped in it: he commonly uses such past participles as 'mistook' or 'forsook' or 'forgot' in place of 'mistaken' or 'forsaken' or 'forgotten', and he will write 'twenty pound' rather than 'twenty pounds'.

But his is not the eighteenth century that might be reconstructed by an historical novelist. It is original, organic, springing straight from the Garfield imagination; though I believe that the work of other writers, and artists, has provided an essential compost. You may well discern something of Stevenson in Garfield's first book, *Jack Holborn* (1964), and something of Dickens everywhere. You may be sure that Garfield knows the work of Fielding and Hogarth, among much else from the eighteenth century itself. There are less obvious writers whose work can fruitfully be considered in relation to his: the great Russian novelists, especially Dostoevsky; even Jane Austen; even Emily Brontë. There are themes that recur: mysteries of origin and identity; the deceptive appearances of good and evil; contrasts of true and false feeling; the precarious survival of compassion and charity in a tempestuous world. These have always been major Garfield preoccupations, and later novels such as *The Prisoners of September* and *The Pleasure Garden* have added some new ones.

Jack Holborn was originally submitted for publication as an adult novel. It was a perceptive editor, Grace Hogarth of Constable, who saw a children's book in it and persuaded Garfield to cut it with that in mind. On the surface it is a tale of piracy, murder, treasure, treachery, shipwreck and ultimate fortune, all in the best traditions of the sea adventure story. And so it will be read by children and by most other readers. There are also two separate questions of identity. One is simple: just who *is* the hero-narrator, the foundling Jack Holborn, so named from the parish in which he was abandoned? The other is disconcerting: how can it be that identical faces cover such different personalities as those of the distinguished Judge and the wicked pirate captain? Confusion between real and apparent good and evil is a frequent Garfield theme; but the device used in *Jack*

Holborn – the introduction of identical twins of opposite character – is crude in comparison with the moral complexity of later
novels. And *Jack Holborn* has other flaws. The story, of which
the first three-quarters are gripping, falls away in the final
quarter; the narrator is brave, generous and well-meaning, but
he is not interesting. Yet *Jack Holborn* shows many of its
author's qualities already strongly developed; the Garfield
style, force and vision are already unmistakable.

Devil-in-the-Fog (1966), the second novel, again revolves at
length around questions of identity. The narrator George Treet,
from being a member of a family of travelling players, is
translated suddenly to the position of heir apparent to Sir John
Dexter, baronet. In the misty grounds of the great house lurks
Sir John's unloving brother, newly cut out of the succession.
But who is the true villain, and is George gentleman or player?
The book shows one clear advance on *Jack Holborn:* the difficulty of making the narrator into an effective character in his
own right is overcome. The artless George, in telling his story,
allows us to see more of him than he can see of himself: we
perceive, for instance, the honest vulgarity that makes him
unacceptable to Sir John as an heir. And here enters another
Garfield theme, that of true and false feeling; for we can contrast
and appraise at their proper values the simple vanity of the
Treets and the chilly pride of Sir John. But the story, though
agreeably melodramatic, is overcomplicated, and not even the
Garfield energy is quite enough to drive it through its own
convolutions and lengthy denouement without loss of pace.
Like *Jack Holborn,* it displays outstanding promise rather than
outstanding achievement.

Smith (1967), the first of Leon Garfield's third-person narra-
tions, was and still remains the most straightforward of his
longer novels. The hero Smith, who doesn't possess such a
luxury as a Christian name, is a twelve-year-old London pick-
pocket who

was a sooty spirit of the violent and ramshackle town, and inhabited
the tumbledown mazes about fat St. Paul's like the subtle air itself. A

rat was a snail beside Smith, and the most his thousand victims ever got of him was the powerful whiff of his passing and a cold draught in their dexterously emptied pockets.

Two moments of pity – for a dying man and for a blind magistrate – get Smith caught up in a whirl of villainy, and set him perilously at odds with a world of thieves, highwaymen, murderers. Over this world loom Newgate Gaol and the gallows. Through it move, side by side, the small, sharp, devious Smith and the upright tragic figure of the blind magistrate; by them wickedness is unmasked and a fortune regained. And the figures of Smith and the magistrate, apparent opposites, are meanwhile moving towards each other, impelled by a growing respect and understanding. Once more there is a puzzle of identity: who is the mysterious Mr Black, and what has become of the long-departed son of the murdered man? There is also the confusion of good and evil; for the respectable young attorney who is paying his attentions to the magistrate's daughter is not what he seems, while it is the third-rate highwayman Lord Tom who saves the sum of things at the cost of his own life. In *Smith* the forward progress of the story is no longer hindered by entanglement in complications; it knows where it is going and drives steadily towards its powerful climax.

Smith, which was serialized on British television, was a successful book, both in literary and commercial terms, and not a difficult one for young people to absorb. Leon Garfield had obviously found his feet, established himself firmly in possession of a congenial and distinctive fictional territory, and overcome the slight weakness of construction which had caused his first two books to lose impetus in their closing chapters. If he had been content to repeat himself with variations, and to refrain from making too many demands either on himself or his readers, he could presumably have enjoyed a relatively easy professional life from that point onwards. But that would not be his way; he has set himself fresh technical problems, gone more deeply into the issues that interest him, and responded to further influences. That is why it is difficult to generalize about his novels as a body of work; each has been very much a new endeavour, requiring to be considered on its own.

Black Jack (1968), with the over-lifesize figure who gives it its title, with its unforgettably macabre opening and its near-apocalyptic end, is an extremely powerful book, 'bigger' than *Smith* and unusual in structure: resembling, one might say, a symphony with dynamic first and last movements and quieter inner ones, rather than a more orthodox novel, in which one might expect to see a more continuous progress, a steadier build-up of tension. Black Jack himself is 'a vast ruffian, nearly seven foot high and broad to match, who'd terrorized the lanes about Knightsbridge till a quart of rum and five police officers laid him low'. A silver tube in his throat cheats the hangman, and cheats the 'Tyburn widow', Mrs Gorgandy, dealer in corpses; for, by the time she's arranged a sale of the body, there's no body to sell. Black Jack is out and about in the reluctant company of young Tolly, draper's apprentice and hero of the story.

But now in the middle third of the book Black Jack withdraws to the wings; the centre of the stage is taken by the love story of Tolly and the young girl from the madhouse, Belle, who travel the lanes together with the well-meaning fairground quack Dr Carmody. Only in the apocalyptic closing chapters – set in London at the time of the great earthquake scare of 1750 – does the giant, chastened in spirit but in full strength of body, come into his own. For, as tremors shake London, and the Northern Lights spread across the sky, and the end of the world is declared to be at hand, it is Black Jack who breaks open the madhouse and helps Belle and Tolly to find their happiness.

The love story of Belle and Tolly – fresh and touching, and a new departure in Leon Garfield's work – makes a striking contrast with the overt or latent violence of the passages in which Black Jack himself is at large; but the book is, I think, less involved with ideas than its author's next novel, *The Drummer Boy* (1970). The boy himself, Charlie Samson, is something of an empty vessel: a receptacle for the hopes, dreams and lost ideals of others, but too innocent and ignorant to be anything positive. With Charlie the story moves from a battlefield on which ten thousand scarlet soldiers have been mown down to London, where the responsible General is trying to save his skin. In thrall to the General's beautiful and apparently dying daughter Sophia, Charlie is ready to perjure himself and shift the General's guilt to a haunted wretch of a scapegoat. He is brought to his senses by the cowardly, fat, sexually ambiguous surgeon Mister Shaw and the common servant girl Charity.

Clearly the book is concerned with the evils of false romanticism. The brief and doubtful glory of the battlefield is a poor exchange for the slow ripening of a lifetime which we see awaiting Charlie in the story's happy ending. The brief and doubtful glory of serving *belle dame sans merci* Sophia and her exalted, hollow father is nothing in comparison with the warmth of an honest wench with twenty pounds in the bank and a loving nature. Again there is the bewildering interchange of good and evil; for the apparently natural love of Charlie for Sophia turns out to be a deadly menace, while the seemingly unnatural love of Mister Shaw for Charlie, though it is hopeless, pathetic, incapable of fruition, is beneficent. It would be possible to see Mister Shaw as the hero of this story: himself the battlefield, with his healing gift at war with half a dozen ignoble purposes.

The Strange Affair of Adelaide Harris is an intricate comedy: the happiest and in many ways the most enjoyable of all the novels. The setting is Dr Bunnion's Academy for the Sons of Gentlefolk and Merchants in early nineteenth-century Brighton; the characters are mainly the Academy's staff and their families. There are also two dreadful pupils, the sturdy but dimwitted Bostock and his friend, the fiendishly-ingenious Harris. Harris's younger sister Adelaide, who gives her name to the story, has only a passive role, being a mere seven weeks old; but from the plan of Bostock and Harris to expose her on the hillside in the hope that she will be suckled by a vixen there follows a sequence of strange, complicated and increasingly hilarious events.

The cast is large, and the action circulates continually among the various characters, but the hero undoubtedly is mild Mr Brett, the classics master, who loves pretty Tizzy Alexander, the arithmetic master's daughter, but is so shy that he can't say a civil word to her. When Tizzy brings tiny Adelaide home, the resultant misunderstanding leads to an affair of honour between her father and her would-be lover Ralph Bunnion; and Mr Brett, whose incapacities include an inability to say 'No', finds himself enlisted as a second by both sides. From this point onwards, matters grow ever more tangled; but the author knows where he is going, and a brilliant unravelling of innumerable strands leaves everything neatly sorted out and Mr Brett and Tizzy happily paired. This is a light-hearted book of many casual joys, among them the naïvely cynical remarks of schoolboy Harris, who shakes Boston's foundations by declaring that 'there ain't no God'.

'But there must be a God,' urged Bostock desperately.
'Why, old friend?'
'Because – because of everything. Look about you, Harris! All the grass and trees and different animals and flowers. Who made them if not God?'
'Somebody else,' said Harris bleakly.

The title of *The Sound of Coaches* is taken from one of the songs in *The Beggar's Opera,* a work with which, in its combination of high spirits and low life, high romance and low cunning, the book has something in common. Sam, brought up by a coachman and his wife, speculates about his real father – a mystery of identity again – and moves from the world of coaching to that of the stage, under the wing of a 'second pa' who may be closer to him than he thinks. The real question of course is not so much who he is as what he is; that's what Sam has to find out. And among his discovered realities is Jenny, the servant girl at the Shakespeare's Head, who is 'bright and current as a worn shilling'. Jenny lies and steals, but in spite of this she has a kind of vulgar honesty and a fine line in earthy rhetoric, which together make her probably Leon Garfield's most memorable and endearing female character.

A Sounding of Storytellers

The Sound of Coaches is mainstream Garfield, and as close as he has come to continuing the straightforward, ebullient line of *Smith*. *The Prisoners of September* is a more sombre and searching book. The great public event on which its action hangs is the French Revolution, and its central incident arises from the massacre of 'enemies of the people' in a Paris prison in September 1792 (hence the title). But it is not 'about' the Revolution: rather, the Revolution is the force under whose pressure the human reactions and interrelations which are the book's real subject-matter take place.

It is a tale of two friends, not of two cities. Lewis, son of the upstart, innocent, new-rich Bostons, goes to Paris and impulsively spends his father's money on rescuing three prisoners – a count, his wife and his daughter – from the revolutionaries. It turns out that he has rescued a swindler who, brought to England, goes on swindling. But Lewis has done nothing worse than make a naïve mistake, and he comes out of it well enough in the end; he is going to marry the Count's daughter and will no doubt live happily ever after. With his childhood friend Richard Mortimer it is another matter. Mortimer, the aristocratic idealist who despises his own class and goes to France to serve the Revolution, becomes the dupe of those who would lead it, for their own ends, into a vicious blind alley of brutal violence; and, driven by his misguided passion, becomes a murderer, perverted and mad. Lewis's is the way of daylight, Richard's the way of darkness; and Richard condemns himself to death. But the key passage of the whole book is when Lewis, long-separated from Richard, goes at the end to see him in gaol. Richard's terrifying despair is matched by Lewis's equally terrifying compassion; there is the beginning of atonement and the flower..ng of a greater love than before. 'I love you,' Richard whispers. 'I love you as I should love Christ.'

These last themes – of darkness and light and their strange interdependence, of love born from the depths and perhaps ambiguous, and of redemption – are not new in Garfield's novels, but have become more prominent and are explored more searchingly in his later work. Though the context is totally different, all can be traced in *The Pleasure Garden*. With this book, and with the series *Garfield's Apprentices* which appeared over the following two years, he returned to eighteenth-century London. The Mulberry Garden is a commercial pleasance which at that time really did exist in Clerkenwell. For the author's purposes it is a place of dreams and pretences and of a curious kind of innocence: a place where the old can pretend to be young, the ugly to be beautiful and the poor to be rich. Its amenities include a dozen arbours for the use of loving couples; but when the garden has closed for the night

out of the low branches and down the sides and backs of the arbours slid and dropped various black creatures, like misshapen fruits. . . The dark creatures, the windfall from the arbours, turned out to be children, human children of supernaturally ragged and filthy appearance. Several of them exhibited cuts and scratches from thorns and broken branches, and it seemed that they'd bled not blood but dirt, that they were dirt all through, that their very bones were grubby and the marrow in them was as black as sin. Only their eyes, the windows of their souls, were bright and gleeful, being composed of a substance that even dirt shrank from. . .

In return for silver sixpences, these infant ruffians disclose the goings-on in the leafy arbours to the Mulberry Gardens management – enormously fat Mrs Bray and tall, thin, white-faced, black-clad Dr Dormann – who then apply blackmail to such lovers as can afford it. Yet it's an honest kind of blackmail: those who submit to it are given a season ticket and thereafter left in peace; they have paid for their pleasure, or their illusion. And all is well in the Mulberry Garden until the night when murder is done there, and amid serpentine complications a mystery must be unravelled.

The figure at the centre of this story is a young clergyman, the Reverend Martin Young, who has a gift of bringing peace and comfort to those around him: a virtuous man, yet not immaculate, for he destroys evidence against a young woman called Fanny whom he thinks to be the murderer. And for this action he is pursued by Dr Dormann, himself an ambiguous character: saint, devil, fallen angel? Martin survives an ultimate encounter with Dormann and the real murderer, and wins through, it seems, to love; for the last of many Biblical references has Fanny reading to him from the Song of Solomon, which 'someone told me, not long ago, is the holiest book in the Scriptures'.

If there is a key to *The Pleasure Garden* it must surely be sought in the Bible. Leon Garfield has expressed some weariness with the Norse and Celtic mythologies now in fictional vogue; he finds them lacking in humanity and says that the Bible is a far richer source, 'incorporating on the one hand the whole range of human experience, on the other hand poetry at its highest level . . . It's not a thing to be made clear and comprehensible; it's a thing to be felt.'[1] It seems safe to say that, in one of its aspects at least, the Pleasure Garden is a Garden of Eden; and it looks very much as though Leon Garfield has rewritten the Fall. Here is his *Paradise Lost*, and perhaps also his *Paradise Regained*, since at the end the Mulberry Garden is still in business; Eden is still open to the innocent, even the seedily innocent. But this is not by a very long way the whole matter of the book, which itself is to be felt rather than to be fully comprehended.

Clearly the Bible is also a major influence in the cycle of twelve stories about London apprentices, each with a different hero or heroine. The stories, covering the months of a year, linked by cross-references and by the reappearances of characters, have appeared individually in England but in fact form a single work. The theme once more is the Light and the Dark: not in the simplistic sense in which these massive abstractions have been used by writers of Tolkienish fantasy to indicate the good and bad sides in some kind of cosmic war. The light has many facets. In *The Lamplighter's Funeral*, the first of the twelve stories, small boy Possul has a disconcerting way of shining his link-boy's torch into the darkest corners, illuminating the depths of misery and degradation. But light in dark places is still

1. Article on Leon Garfield by John Rowe Townsend, *Guardian*, 5 May 1976.

light. *Mirror, Mirror* is a small gem of a book about a mirror-frame carver's apprentice who is tormented by the pretty but cruel daughter of his master, until the day comes when he turns the mirror on her and shows her what she is. Her name is Lucinda: what else?

The theme of redemption is handled with audacious brilliance in *The Cloak*, in which two pawnbrokers' apprentices, who make money by re-pawning pledged items with each other, are caught out over a black silk cloak with the embroidered text 'I know that my Redeemer liveth.' A stranger does indeed turn up and demand to redeem it, to their discomfiture. In *Moss and Blister*, the midwife and her assistant, 'a tall thin girl with sticking-out ears and saucer eyes, who flapped and stalked after stubby Moss like a loose umbrella', are convinced that on Christmas Eve they will be present in a professional capacity at the Second Coming, and there is indeed a baby to be delivered in the inn yard, but for a very good reason it cannot be He. As is inevitable with a long sequence, there is some unevenness, but the achievement as a whole is remarkable. In *Tom Titmarsh's Devil*, the series reaches its most profound and fearful depths with the mysterious Mr Match's soon-to-be-banned book *Thine is the Kingdom*. Mr Match has been shown by a link-boy the most dreadful sights of the London slums (a cross-reference to *The Lamplighter's Funeral*), and describes how in a dream he heard a dead man preach a sermon in a church of bone:

In the beginning, whispered the sermon, in the very beginning, that is, God made the devil, and that was His greatest creation. When He made the devil, He made Himself; because before there was the devil, there was no god. Before there was evil, there was no good. Then He made darkness to make light; because without darkness, there can be no light. Nothing can exist of itself alone.

He thought of guilt, so that He might create innocence. He caused Cain to kill Abel; he caused Judas to betray Christ. Without guilt there is no innocence; without agony there is no joy. . .

So the sermon went on, heaping paradox on paradox, even as the dead were piled on top of each other, as the author, by these strange and wayward means, struggled to answer the questions in his own tormented heart. He was trying as best he knew to come to terms with all the cruelties and miseries he'd seen in the night.

No wonder the Bishop, visiting the shop where this book and also his own sermons are sold, wants such 'blasphemous godless rubbish' burned by the public hangman. It is a supreme irony, and a marvel of authorial ingenuity, that the hangman's apprentice, being illiterate, burns the Bishop's sermons instead.

It is possible to draw from each of these books a text and an interpretation. But it would be wrong to give the impression that they are solemn or harrowing, unlikely to give enjoyment to children or anyone else. There is also, and as a rule more obviously, the Garfield humour and inventiveness, and the constant delight of the Garfield way with words. Miss Sparrow, the printer's devil in *Tom Titmarsh* for instance, 'was so liberally daubed with printer's ink that put her in a press and you might have had fifty clear impressions without the need for re-inking her once'.

The books discussed here are not the whole body of Leon Garfield's work up to the time of writing. In addition to some shorter books which there is not space to mention, he has written two splendid ghost stories. *Mister Corbett's Ghost* (1968) is about a boy who wishes his harsh master dead and appears to get his wish, but then cannot be rid of the pitiful, lingering spectre; *The Ghost Downstairs* is a variation on the Faust legend, but turns out to be a salvation rather than a damnation of Faust. Leon Garfield has also collaborated with Edward Blishen in the reworking of Greek myth and legend in *The God Beneath the Sea* (1970) and *The Golden Shadow* (1973). Both books have received severe condemnation as well as praise. The most common ground of censure has been a prose style that was thought excessively florid. In principle I think this complaint inappropriate. English prose since Dryden's day has been an instrument designed for practical everyday use; it is not equal to recording the deeds of gods and Titans. Possibly Leon Garfield is the only writer who could bring to it a necessary grandiloquence. It cannot be maintained however that the books are consistently successful, stylistically; they take a perilous course along which the line between very good and very bad can be a fine one. Here is Zeus dealing with Hera:

He hung her in the sky with golden bracelets from her wrists and golden anvils to drag her ankles down. Hers was a royal fate. Her raging beauty stared down on the world, while her rich black hair flew across the face of the shaken moon. Stars pricked her fingertips, but such was the scope of her pride that she scorned to clench her hands and wore the stars like sharply splintered jewels; while in the northern sky her black and scarlet gown hung down in deep, unmoving folds. There she remained until Zeus's anger was spent.

Which side of the line is that? I am not prepared to answer in a sentence. Adequate discussion of the two books would obviously require not only a full stylistic analysis but an examination in detail of the treatment of specific themes of Greek mythology, and the present short essay does not give scope for this. Indeed, one feels generally constrained in trying to deal briefly with so productive and various a writer. I have not had time to explore, as I would wish to do, Garfield's extraordinary and significant choice of imagery, his penchant for the macabre, his shrewd yet sympathetic eye for roguery, inconsistency and self-deception, his wit, his occasional tenderness and poetry.

'Rich and strange' was the phrase I used in *A Sense of Story* to describe Leon Garfield's talent, and it remains no less apt after his second seven years. The fertility of his creative imagination and his commanding way with words are as evident as before; his humanity and charity become more obvious as his scope increases. His faults are on the right side, and arise from going too far rather than from falling short. My expectation of further achievement is as confident as ever.

Leon Garfield writes:

Having just completed writing a comedy, and watched a reader actually laugh aloud over the typescript, I feel I never want to write anything else but comedy. Tragedy may purge the emotions but comedy sustains them.

This is no easy option; nor does it preclude the depicting of human feelings in all their painful truth. Indeed, nobody ought to laugh *in* a comedy, only *at* it. Characters in comedies are confronted with the most terrible situations: they ache for forsaken love; they weep for lost opportunities; and they suffer for their sins in the most complicated way. They can make no sense of the world and wish they were dead. The reader alone, seeing everything, can make sense of it; and, with luck, is glad that everyone's alive.

Perhaps I'm setting too high a value on comedy? It's possible; but it's worth bearing in mind that somebody stole Charlie Chaplin's body while nobody, so far as I know, has made the slightest effort to nick the remains of any Prime Minister.

So now I'll try to think of something funny; and, believe me, nothing is more calculated to promote anguish and gloom.

Alan Garner

Alan Garner was born in 1935 and was educated at Alderley Edge Primary School, Manchester Grammar School, and Magdalen College, Oxford. He was a keen athlete at school and won many championships for his county as a sprinter. He left Oxford to become a full-time writer and now lives with his wife and children in an ancient cottage in Cheshire. His principal books are Elidor *(1965),* The Owl Service *(1967) and* Red Shift *(1973).*

Alan Garner has long been one of the most discussed of contemporary British writers for children. He is also one of the few whose names are known to some extent among adults outside the literary world. All short-lists of leading children's authors include his name: a name which carries with it associations of high esteem and exceptional brilliance.

This reputation has not been achieved by high output. Between 1960 and 1978 he published the five novels and four briefer stories discussed here, and some minor work, including a children's nativity play, *Holly from the Bongs* (1966), and the text of a picture book, *The Breadhorse* (1975), illustrated by Albin Trowski. But his books, though few, have had an extraordinarily powerful impact; they have been felt and not forgotten.

The five novels can all be broadly – very broadly – described as fantasy, and all are rooted, to varying degrees, in ancient legend and story. A full-scale study of Garner's work would call for much research among Celtic, Scandinavian and other mythology and in widespread fields of folklore, anthropology, history and prehistory. I have not the space here for any such

81

study, nor am I qualified to produce one. And this may not be entirely a disadvantage. Although a scholarly approach would have its interest, I am not at all sure that the detailed exploration of sources is required or even desirable before attempting a brief critical assessment. For an author is only entitled, and would only wish, to take credit for his sources to the extent to which he has absorbed them and incorporated them effectively into his own work. And when he has done so they are not 'sources' any more; they are part of himself.

Because Garner's novels have come out at fairly long intervals, they show their differences – and the author's development – more clearly than do the works of more prolific writers. Alan Garner has never stood still. The novels have grown less complicated but more complex, less crowded but more intricately ramified, and more demanding. *The Weirdstone of Brisingamen* (1960) was Garner's first book; it is rapid, crowded, and an easy, gripping read. *Red Shift* (1973) is his latest full-length novel at the time of writing; it is complex and intricate, and it makes heavy demands on the reader's intelligence, concentration and background knowledge. Even a tolerably satisfactory reading requires an ability to make swift imaginative leaps, pick up allusions, and expand in the mind what the author may merely have indicated in a few brief words. There has been much argument about whether it is a book for children or young people at all.

When *The Weirdstone of Brisingamen* first appeared, it was hinted that Garner was indebted to J. R. R. Tolkien. In fact he did not then know Tolkien's work. The great difference between Tolkien and early Garner is that Tolkien creates a world of magic apart from our own while Garner brings magic into our own world, here and now. This is an important principle with him. He wrote in a *New Statesman* review:

If we are in Eldorado, and we find a mandrake, then O.K., so it's a mandrake: in Eldorado anything goes. But, by force of imagination compel the reader to believe that there is a mandrake in a garden in Mayfield Road, Ulverston, Lancs, then when you pull up that

Alan Garner

mandrake it is really going to scream; and possibly the reader will, too.[1]

Garner's magic in the early books is kept in constant, breathless use, and is enhanced and made more credible by the solidity of his settings. In *The Weirdstone* and its sequel, *The Moon of Gomrath* (1963), the background is the Cheshire countryside around Alderley Edge: firm, hard, topographically accurate. It is so plainly authentic that it gives the illusion of authenticating the story; though in any case the reader is given little time in which to stop and doubt.

Two children, Colin and Susan, find, in *The Weirdstone,* that they are in possession of the magic stone that guards the company of knights who will one day wake to save the world. They lose the stone to evil forces, recover it, and make a perilous dash across country to put it in the hands of the good magician Cadellin. (The story is, of course, a pendant to existing legend, and Cadellin is known by other names.) On each side, new ranks of creatures are called successively into the struggle: dwarfs, goblins, warlocks, scarecrows, a lady of the lake, a fairy horse, pin-headed troll women. Sometimes one has the impression that ever more properties are being brought out of a bottomless wardrobe; at other times it seems as if a game of high-speed chess is going on. There is not much subtlety, but the cliffhanging excitement is intense, and not even Garner has surpassed it.

In *The Moon of Gomrath*, though the driving force behind the story is no greater, the quality of imagination and the poetry with which Garner invests his traditional materials are greatly enhanced. The action breaks into two parts. In the first, Susan is possessed by an ancient, formless mischief called the Brollachan, and to free her Colin must find and pluck a magic flower; in the second, Colin is held prisoner by a vengeful witch, the Morrigan, and eventually rescued. But there is much more to it than that. The Brollachan, if I understand matters

1. Alan Garner, 'Real Mandrakes in Real Gardens', *New Statesman,* 1 November 1968.

correctly, is a manifestation of the Old Evil, against which the cerebral High Magic of Cadellin is too delicate a weapon. There is nothing for it but to call in the Old Magic: a fierce, elemental magic of sun and moon, earth and blood, surviving from crueller times. It is the Old Magic that draws Colin by moonlight along the old straight track to find the vital flower. The High Magic of thoughts and spells has held the Old Magic in check, but now it has been disturbed; and under the moon of Gomrath, when the Old Magic sleeps most lightly, the children are instrumental in releasing it. And although in the end the Old Evil is defeated, the Old Magic rides dangerously free.

There is a crucial moment in which the children, bringing fire to an ancient mound on the Eve of Gomrath, arouse three warrior-horsemen: at first unstable as pictures in flame, but becoming solid, real and terrible.

They were dressed all in red: red were their tunics, and red their cloaks; red their eyes, and red their long manes of hair bound back with circlets of red gold; three red shields on their backs, and three red spears in their hands; three red horses under them, and red was the harness. Red were they all, weapons and clothing and hair, both horses and men.

This is the Wild Hunt; and in the way it is let loose there seems to be a suggestion of the loosing of wild fire. Yet the power of the Old Magic is associated above all with moonlight. By moonlight Colin seeks and finds the magic flower; by moonlight the Wild Hunt is aroused; Colin's imprisonment is in a ruined house that by moonlight alone becomes whole. In *The Moon of Gomrath* the poetry and potency of magic are matched.

In his third novel, *Elidor* (1965), for the first time, Garner separates the magical country from the everyday world. Elidor's position in time and space is a question of metaphysics rather than of cosmology, for acts in one world can be reflected in the other. Four children, exploring a slum clearance area in the back streets of Manchester, find themselves translated to the once green, now blighted, land of Elidor. Their role there is to fulfil the ancient prophecy of the Starved Fool and restore light and life to the land. After a brief visit, shadowed by menace, they return to Manchester, bringing with them for safekeeping the Treasures of Elidor, in which its life partly resides. Roland has a spear, David a sword, Nicholas a golden stone, Helen a pearl-rimmed bowl. In the daily world the Treasures become mere bits of junk – except that they have disconcerting effects on electrical equipment. The children bury them in their suburban garden; and now the interactions of our world and Elidor intensify until the spectacular climax in which a unicorn gallops through slum streets, and the Song of Findhorn is heard, and a sunburst sweeps Elidor with colour as the horned beast dies with its head in Helen's lap.

The sources of *Elidor*, the ideas that went into it, are many. If there is one special key, I am fairly sure it lies in Jessie Weston's book *From Ritual to Romance*, which links the Golden Bough with the Grail legend, and is further linked in *Elidor* with the myth of the unicorn. The waste land of Elidor is the waste land which gives T. S. Eliot's poem its title. It is the male pro-creative act that renews life and that takes place in the dying Song of Findhorn; it is no mere incidental detail that Helen's treasure is the bowl – or grail – and that it breaks when the unicorn lays its head in her lap.

Few readers, and probably no child, will recognize the under-lying material; nor is it particularly important either to them or to a brief appraisal of the book. The question is whether it has been absorbed; whether, unknown to the reader, its power has come through and is now Garner's. It seems to me that it has, and that the ending of *Elidor* has a splendour which is totally intrinsic. But I do not think the book as a whole is fully successful. Part of the trouble lies in the land of Elidor itself. After the children's initial visit we see practically nothing of it; we do not know what is going on. There are hints that evil is at work, but what evil we never learn. The trouble may be that nothing really *can* happen there; it is the waste land, the dead land waiting for life. And the children themselves do not match the size of the story. As Elidor's saviours they have been the subject of prophecy there; their likenesses appear in an old and treasured book 'written so long ago that we have only legend to tell us about it'. Yet they are quite ordinary and rather uninteresting. So indeed were Colin and Susan in the two earlier books, but there it did not matter so much; Colin and Susan were just 'a boy and girl', and could even be seen as blank spaces into which readers could insert themselves. One might expect more from the four who save Elidor; one might also expect, in this generally more subtle novel, that they would be changed by the things that happen to them; but it is hard to perceive any development in their characters as the story unfolds.

The deepening and strengthening of the human element in *The Owl Service* (1967) is in fact a key difference between that book and the three earlier novels just discussed. To my mind *The Owl Service* shows a new maturity and authority; it is the work of a man who has mastered his craft and knows just what he is about. The theme is characteristic of Garner: the irruption of old legend into modern life. But this time the author is concerned with the emotional realities of a situation existing here and now. In earlier books, the people were little more than pawns; the power lay in external forces. In *The Owl Service*, the legend and its re-enactments are in their true place as phenomena arising out of the nature of humanity rather than working on it from outside. People – unthinking, vulnerable, little knowing what harm they can do to themselves and others – carry the potentiality for disaster within them. They also carry within them the potentiality for avoiding disaster.

The legend behind and within *The Owl Service* is the story from the Fourth Branch of the Mabinogion which tells how the magician Gwydion made a wife of flowers for Lleu Llaw Gyffes, and how the wife betrayed her husband and took Gronw Pebyr for her lover. Gronw was killed by Lleu, and in punishment for the wife's sin Gwydion turned her into Blodeuwydd, the owl, the bird of prey to which other birds are hostile.

Garner's novel is set in a valley supposed to be the same setting as that of the old story, in which the agony of Blodeuwydd builds up from time to time over the years and forces its way out afresh in similar, recurrent situations. In the

Alan Garner

big house are Alison and Roger, young English people who have been made stepbrother and stepsister by the marriage of Alison's mother to Roger's father; and mixing uneasily with them on first-name terms of not-quite-equality is Gwyn, the housekeeper's son, the Welsh grammar-school boy with a huge chip on his shoulder. With these three the vicious triangle re-forms; the power of Blodeuwydd – 'she wants to be flowers, but you make her owls' – grows, throbs nearer, builds to unbearable tension, and comes to wild release in the last few pages. Disaster is at hand. When the drama was last enacted, a generation ago, it ended in death. This time the worst is averted; and it is averted by insensitive, unimaginative English Roger, not by the passionate, intelligent Welsh boy Gwyn. The few necessary words of forgiveness and understanding are more than the tortured Gwyn can offer.

The supernatural is used sparingly but to great effect. *The Owl Service* is, as I have indicated, essentially a human story, and if he had been so minded Garner could have done without any element of fantasy at all. The memory of the legend, the knowledge that this valley was its setting and that the tragedy had recurred here more than once, a sense of impending and barely-escapable doom: these surely would have sufficed. This is not to say that the author ought to have *made* them suffice. People must write their books in their own ways.

Among the themes of *The Owl Service* is that of relationships between the generations and, specifically, the damage that possessive parents can do to their children. Another is that of 'Welsh and English', with all that the words connote. Gwyn and his embittered mother Nancy are of the 'inferior' race, the occupied country, whereas Alison and Roger and their parents are of the one-time ascendancy. The dialogue is subtle, quick, accurate, full of nuances, and is a great advance on Garner's previous work. The characterization is still a little patchy. To me it seems that Gwyn and his mother Nancy are the living and breathing likenesses of real people, that the feeble *bonhomie* and underlying nullness of Roger's father Clive are wholly credible, and that Alison's mother Margaret is outlined with remarkable

87

clarity considering that she never actually appears. But Alison and Roger have an ordinariness which, though no doubt intended, leaves them like the children in *Elidor* unequal to their parts in the story. They are not strong enough, not positive enough, to make two corners of this eternal and passionate triangle. The book has to carry them; fortunately it has power enough to do so. I have said and still say that *The Owl Service* is – against formidable competition – the most remarkable novel to appear on a British children's list in the 1960s.

Six years went by between publication of *The Owl Service* and of Garner's next novel *Red Shift*. It had been eagerly awaited and gave rise to a great deal of sometimes-baffled discussion. Scientifically, the phrase 'red shift', if I understand it correctly, refers to a change in the spectrum associated with a retreating light source. This phenomenon, observed in stars, gave rise to the theory of the expanding universe. It has a bearing on relativity and on the nature of time. In the context of the book the phrase has other associations as well, but as a beginning I think it may be taken to imply that time is not the simple progression which we assume for the purposes of our daily lives. It is conceivable that events in different times may in a sense be simultaneous, just as events in different places may be simultaneous. And Garner weaves intricately together stories from three different periods, moving frequently between them and finally fusing them all together at the end of the book.

The first of the novel's three strands is a contemporary strand: a story of young love in difficulty. Tom and Jan face physical separation, possessive and poisonous interference from the boy's mother, and psychological problems arising from Tom's mental condition. He is brilliant but unstable – the instability itself being apparently in part a result of parental possessiveness and incomprehension. The other two strands are at different removes in the past. In the first of them a youngster called Macey is among a small band of Roman ex-legionaries 'going tribal' in Britain; in the second, Thomas is one of the villagers who take refuge in Barthomley Church, in Cheshire, during English Civil War fighting. Macey and Thomas, like present-day Tom, are inadequate, unstable characters; and each is associated with a girl whose role is protective and with whom he appears not to play a man's part sexually.

Macey and Thomas are obviously *alter egos* of Tom. Whether their experiences are 'really' happening to each of them separately, or are psychotic hallucinations of present-day Tom, or are happening to Tom in a series of time-shifts, are questions which do not have to be decided; the mind is capable of accommodating more than one possibility at once. The 'earlier' events cannot be solely hallucinatory, however, for the Barthomley massacre took place as a matter of historical fact in 1643, and several persons named in the Garner text were among those killed. Indeed, the immediate cause of the massacre was that one of the villagers who had fled to the church fired on a marauding soldier – just as Garner's Thomas does.

The novel moves among these three times and also among three locations. The first is Mow Cop, a hill in Cheshire where the ex-legionaries make their headquarters and which they find is a sacred place to the tribesmen: 'It's the netherstone of the world. The skymill turns on it to grind stars.' The second is Barthomley; the third is Rudheath, a few miles away, where modern Tom lives with his parents on a caravan site. Tom and Jan are drawn to Barthomley and Mow Cop; and the characters in both of the other two strands find sanctuary at Rudheath and are involved in violence at Barthomley.

A fourth significant place appears only in the contemporary story, not having existed at the times of the earlier ones. This is Crewe Station – epitome of transience – where the lovers meet. The strands are interwoven not only by the recurrence of the same places but by the appearance in each story of a stone axe which even in the earliest episode is described as 'the axe from way back'. Macey hides it at Barthomley, where Thomas finds it; Thomas is to build it into a house at Mow Cop, to be found by Tom. To entwine the times and people still more, there are forward perceptions by both Macey and Thomas, and conscious anachronisms: words from *King Lear* are heard in the tribal story; the ex-legionaries speak the language of G.I.s.

The 'red' of the phrase 'red shift' may be taken to carry its obvious connotations of violence and bloodshed. In the two 'early' stories the violence is bloody massacre. Macey goes berserk at Barthomley, Thomas fires the shot that provokes the assault. In the contemporary story there is no overt violence, but it is on the tower at Barthomley that Tom and Jan become lovers; and there is no joy in it, then or after. The impression is overwhelming that Tom does violence to their love and, even though she consents, in truth violates her. In the early stories it seems that Macey and Thomas survive; each retains the girl he is with, although others have possessed them; and each saves the axe to be found again. But modern Tom is a disastrous person. He sells the axe; betrays Jan; murders love. The ending for this couple appears to be one of total breakdown and failure.

A last parallel that must be pointed out is between the story of Tom and Jan and the ballad of Tam Lin, in which the lovers are Tam and Janet. Tom surely is a shape-shifter if ever there was one, and Jan tries with all her might to hold on to him. But she is a Janet who fails.

There are other aspects of the book that I have not discussed, and some no doubt that I am unaware of. I do not seek to supply a crib; and nobody, not even the author, can provide a definitive exegesis of a book. Obviously *Red Shift* is a complex structure. Artistically, is it a sound one? I am not sure. For all the ingenuity with which the three stories are woven together, I feel that the relationship of the earlier two to the contemporary one is not fully organic. This last, which is the outer and clearly the principal story, stands up perfectly well without the others. They add, but they do not inhere. They could be removed from the book and the outer story would still be there. And it would be seen to be rather a banal little story, no better than many other portrayals of young love and worse than some. The highly intelligent yet ineffectual and ultimately destructive Tom is probably Garner's most successful characterization so far, but his dreadful parents come close to being stereotypes, and even Jan does not emerge clearly as a person. Her account of her previous brief affair with a married man is almost novelettish. The dialogue has what Eleanor Cameron, writing of *The Owl Service,* described as a staccato beat giving the impression of choppiness.[2] (This can, however, be brilliantly effective at times. On the day when Tom has learned of Jan's former lover, one can clearly hear his silent inward screaming beneath the ordinary words.)

In spite of what seem sizeable flaws, *Red Shift* comes across as a strong, disturbing and memorable novel. Possibly Garner has turned his main weakness into a strength. In past books, as I have already indicated, one has felt that his characters did not match the size of their stories. In *Red Shift,* Tom, his girl and his parents match the size of *their* story, because it is not a big one; it is not the size of the whole book. The image left in my mind is a visual image: an image of small, vulnerable present-day people with great black shadows of the past looming over them. This may not have been the author's aim, but I think it is his achievement.

Who will be the readers of *Red Shift*? I do not think they can be, in large numbers, the children and early teenagers who were Alan Garner's original audience. The emotional and literary experience required, the attention with which the book must be read, are likely to deter almost all children and most adolescents. Garner makes no concessions. But he has fulfilled the author's duty of writing the best book he can. In the long run *Red Shift,* like other books which have something to say, will find its appropriate audience, whatever that may be.

A question of readership also arises over the four linked stories which Garner published in 1976, 1977 and 1978. They are a quartet of brief books printed in large type, and look as if intended for children of the middle years, perhaps eight to ten or eleven. But they have no strong plot line, no easy appeal; and probably they require a more patient, thoughtful and mature reader than one might suppose at first sight. The four – in order of the events they describe, not in order of publication – are *The Stone Book* (1976), *Granny Reardun* (1977), *The Aimer Gate*

2. Eleanor Cameron, 'The Owl Service: a Study', *Wilson Library Bulletin*, December 1969.

(1978) and *Tom Fobble's Day* (1977). They are linked by the names and family descents of the people in them and by their shared setting in a corner of rural Cheshire; linked, too, by the theme that runs through them all. They are about crafts and craftsmen, their tools and materials, the choice of a trade, and the handing down of skill (and strength and wisdom) from generation to generation. Each has a boy or girl in the foreground; each covers the events of only one significant day; but among them the four books span five generations. Mary's father in *The Stone Book* is the grandfather of Joseph in *Granny Reardun*; Joseph in turn is the father of Robert in *The Aimer Gate* and the grandfather of William in *Tom Fobble's Day*.

Mary's father is a mason who has built most of the village and is now finishing the church spire. *The Stone Book* begins with Mary climbing up ladder after ladder to take him his baggin (lunch). He sits her on the weathercock and spins her gloriously (if, to the reader, vertiginously) around. It's a day to remember, but Mary is not quite content. She wishes she could read, or at least have a prayer-book to carry to church like Lizzie Allman and Annie Leah. And then Father takes her way down below ground, through tunnels made by miners, to a narrow maze which she alone, holding an Ariadne's-thread of silk, can traverse, until she comes to a cave where there is a picture of a great bull drawn on the rock wall: a secret which only successive generations of her family see. And after that Father makes her a book of stone which he says is 'better than a book you can open'; and Mary 'sat by the fire and read the stone book that had in it all the stories of the world and the flowers of the flood'.

Sermons in stone, one cannot help thinking. Stone holds history, and stone, unlike ink on paper, can tell no lies. It's a beautifully told and balanced story; its two halves are Mary's climb into the sky and descent into the earth; it is full of echoes and resonances. Yet I confess I find it the least sympathetic of the four books, largely because it leaves me worrying over an obvious but surely important point. Father can read. Mary wants to read, too, and one feels quite passionately that she should be taught to do so, not fobbed off with an imitation book. Whatever wisdom may reside in stone and in the mason's craft, a stone book is no substitute for a real one; indeed, it is a contradiction in terms, almost a perversion of the nature of stone.

The other three books, though rich in implication, are simpler and, I think, better. In *Granny Reardun* Joseph, grandson of the Robert who is Mary's father, is in his last day at school, and doesn't want to follow in the mason's craft. He wants to be a smith, because he needs to be different from dominant Grandfather and because a smith is 'aback of everything'; nobody can make anything without tools made by the smith. Joseph finds it hard to tell Grandfather his intention, but when he summons the courage to do so Grandfather takes it, triumphantly. Granny Reardun, by the way, is not a person. Joseph is a 'granny reardun', because his grandmother brought him up.

The Aimer Gate is another title that needs explaining. In dialect the phrase denotes a more direct way, and there's an implication that Uncle Charlie, a soldier in the First World War, will take a short cut to the end of the human journey. This book has if anything less story than any of the others, but there are some exceptionally fine descriptive passages in it. One of them tells of three men scything together and synchronizing their swing because 'if they ever got out of time the blades would cut flesh and bone'. In another a boy climbs high inside a steeple built by the mason who built the church spire in *The Stone Book*, and finds that inside the very top of the steeple the stone is as smooth and true as anywhere else, though it will never be seen.

Tom Fobble's Day, however, is surely the most masterly of the four. It is now the time of the Second World War. William is the grandson of Joseph, the granny reardun who became a smith. A bigger boy has 'Tom Fobbled' (taken) William's sledge and crashed it. And Grandad, on his last working day and it seems the last day of his life, makes William a new sledge. We are told in absorbing detail of the making and the materials. As William sledges downhill, 'he was not alone on a sledge. There was a line, and he could feel it. It was a line through hand and eye, block, forge and loom to the hill. He owned them all: and they owned him.' And at the very end, when Grandad it seems is dead, William is back on the hill, sledging again: 'he sledged sledged sledged for the black and glittering night and the sky flying on fire and the expectation of snow'.

Though I have, as indicated, a reservation about *The Stone Book*, I have no doubt that the quartet as a whole is a fine achievement. The sense of landscape, of people, of the passage of time but the continuity of families and crafts, is marvellously sure and solid; voices ring true and clear with the vigour and dignity of the common folk. In *Red Shift* it was still possible to feel a lack of depth and sympathy in Garner's portrayal of people, and to wonder whether this would turn out to be a crucial limitation of his talent. But no such lack is felt in the quartet; there is more humanity here than in any of his previous work. 'He is always likely to do something one would not have guessed at until it was there,' I wrote in 1971; and these last four books are a good instance. Alan Garner's potentiality is obviously still great, and there is still no telling what he will do next. Whatever it is, it will be eagerly awaited.

Alan Garner

Alan Garner said in the course of an interview with Aidan Chambers, published in *Signal*, September 1978:

I find that most university English graduates I speak to are now journalists – too many for it to be coincidence – and they have admitted to me that they wanted to be creative writers, not journalists. I'm not saying that journalism is worse, it's just different. But they were aware of the corpus of English literature and they felt there wasn't anything left to say. That is both true and stupid, at the same time. I was trained in the schools of Latin and Greek. At the age of eighteen, I was also introduced as an extra subject to English. I found nothing at all that was relevant to me in twentieth-century novels, compared with the relevance that I found in Greek plays that were over two thousand years old. I remember wondering why that should be so, that somebody should have written in Greece over two thousand years ago in such a way that it helped me to come to terms with the way my girl-friend's mother was behaving.

But no novel that I picked up was relevant to me at all. When I actually settled down to write, I thought, This is a very difficult job – so I may as well try to get it as near perfect as the best Greeks did, because it's not going to be much harder. It's going to be very difficult to write badly; it won't be much harder to write well. I tried to find out by going back to the Greek texts. It just happened to be Greek. Any language, I'm certain, would do it. The question was, What was it that made Greek drama universally relevant? The answer seemed to be that the man stayed with the story until it could be said in those words and no others and certainly no more; everything was down to the bone.

The modern novels I had rejected I found were being written by over-literate abstract minds for other literate abstract minds, and I had had enough of that. There was nobody saying to me, 'I love you'. There was nothing really basic, nothing worked through, suffered, resolved. I found very little catharsis in the writing. Mind you, I didn't read a lot of it because my bias was towards the Greek. I knew where to go in my academic skills to find the quintessential nature of writing.

95

So I'm not denying that it exists in English of the twentieth century. I'm saying that I knew where to get it more purely for me. . .

By my mid–twenties, I was aware a) that it was difficult to write anyway, so it was worth hanging on in case you could write well enough to be very good; and b) that there was something missing, and I couldn't find it. Another strand through all the books has been an instinctive searching out of the concrete culture that I had to be removed from in order to be educated. Which is raising a political point, but I think it's one that we don't realize often enough, that the first–generation grammar–school boy from a working–class home, especially if he's of high intelligence, is as much a social problem as the educationally sub–normal. . .

What is it that happens to them?

In my experience one of three things. There is a snapping of the elastic, and the emergent creative intelligence shrivels back into the restrictive narrow confines of the working–class culture, which has become narrow and restrictive by history and also by the widening of the horizon for that child. So the child suffers and becomes a bitter and cynical adult. That is the commonest form. The next one, which is a bridge between accommodating oneself to both cultures, is to become an élitist in the worst sense, which means becoming a bigger rat than any other rat in the race by using all the cunning of one's background. The third way, which is the one I experienced, was to find that the elastic had snapped, but that I couldn't shrivel back into the family. My momentum was such that I shrivelled away from them. It was mutual. My family could not absorb me and I could not bear the pain of saying, in some way, usually emotionally: I'm sorry, I can't be what your preconception would have me be.

I can see all that operating in The Owl Service *and* Red Shift.

Yes.

Is The Stone Book *sequence a kind of — the cliché would be 'coming to terms with'; I'm going to use two other words — forgiveness and redemption of that?*

If I had used those words I think it would have been genuinely precious and pretentious. You've used them. If it's true, I'm very glad. That is certainly something that I hope has come from it. It was not the intent.

Virginia Hamilton

Virginia Hamilton was born in Yellow Springs, Ohio, in 1936, and was educated there and at Ohio State University. She lived for a time in New York, where she met and married Arnold Adoff, but they and their two children have now returned to live in Yellow Springs. Virginia Hamilton's first children's book was Zeely *(1967), and the books that have followed include* The House of Dies Drear *(1968),* The Planet of Junior Brown *(1971) and* Arilla Sun Down *(1976). Her novel* M. C. Higgins the Great *(1974) received the Newbery Medal, the* Boston Globe-Horn Book *Award and the National Book Award.*

I feel more hesitant in writing about Virginia Hamilton than about anyone else in the present book. This is not because she is particularly obscure or difficult; I do not think she is. Take her stories at their face value and they are usually quite simple, quite easy to follow. (*Arilla Sun Down*, it is true, moves back and forth in time, but this ought not to cause any difficulty to an intelligent older child, or adult, with any experience of novel-reading or the cinema.) The problem is that the essence of her work is subtle and elusive, difficult to pin down on the page.

There are writers whose books are 'closed'; what appears in black and white is exactly what they have to say. Their goods are all in the shop window, ticketed and priced. There are others whose books are 'open': the reader is left to draw the inferences, make the connections, provide the interpretation. Virginia Hamilton's books are exceptionally open in this sense. Even at their simplest, her stories are capable of extension; they contain more than is expressed in their words. They cast shadows, and the shadows can vary according to the light the reader brings to them. One is reluctant therefore to offer a hard-and-fast interpretation or assessment. In dealing with an 'open' book, it may be that a critic's most useful contribution is to indicate rather than to appraise; to offer perceptions rather than judgements. It is stultifying, faced with such work, to tease out unambiguous meaning; and where children are concerned it is particularly limiting to the imagination and inimical to the pleasure of reading to insist that they should 'understand' a book in this one-dimensional way. A book makes its own statements, and can hold more than one meaning at the same time.

According to a biographical note by Paul Heins, Virginia Hamilton 'often feels that she is a symbolist'.[1] Without going into the historical intricacies of defining symbolism, one can certainly say that as the term is commonly used nowadays there is a great deal of it in her books. She remarked on this, humorously, in her Newbery Medal acceptance speech for *M. C. Higgins the Great* in 1975. After telling how she burst in on her editor, Susan Hirschman, with the news that 'I had this wild, barefoot youth atop a forty-foot steel pole on the side of a mountain called Sarah's,' she described a further meeting at which she expressed gloom over the prospects of finishing the book.

I anguished and protested to her that this time the book defied solution or completion. How do I write, I worried, when all of my subjects upon creation immediately suggest intangible objects? And I said to Susan, 'How do I keep mountains, rivers, and, yes, black people from turning into myths or emblems of themselves? They are somehow born on the page too large,' I said, 'and no sooner do I put them there all together than the river becomes The-One-That-Has-to-be-Crossed; the mountain is The-One-That's-Got-to-be-Climbed; and my people? A mere symbol of human STRUGGLE, in capital letters, *Against Adversity,* in italics. And that would be playing them cheap,' I said.

1. Paul Heins, biographical note on Virginia Hamilton, *Horn Book,* August 1975, reprinted in *Newbery and Caldecott Medal Books, 1966–1975* (The Horn Book Inc., 1975), pp. 137–40.

And half a minute later Miss Hamilton was (endearingly) mocking herself in reporting her editor's reaction.

'What about the pole?' she [Susan Hirschman] asked.
'What about it?'
'What's *it* a symbol of?'
'It's . . . just what the kid sits on?' I asked tentatively.
'But why doesn't he "just" sit on the mountain or on the porch; why a forty-foot pole on the side of a mountain?'
'Well, it's not his mountain,' I said, feeling unaccountably annoyed, 'it's Sarah's . . . but the pole belongs to him, and that's why he sits on it.'[2]

So the pole, it seems, was not intended to be symbolic; yet surely it became so, willy-nilly, because of the way Miss Hamilton's imagination works. It seems safe to say that when M. C. Higgins is sitting atop the pole he is riding high, he is rising above his environment, he is holding a brilliant and confident though precarious balance. The pole indeed is obviously the throne of M. C. Higgins the Great. . . Like Virginia Hamilton herself in the remarks just quoted, I am not being deadly serious; but – again, I think, like her – I am not entirely joking, either. I am reminded of Helen Cresswell's remark in *A Sense of Story*: 'Carefully worked-out symbolism is almost always cliché. You don't choose symbols – they choose you.'[3]

With Virginia Hamilton, more than with many writers, it is helpful to have a personal context for the author. She is black. Her maternal grandfather, Levi Perry, was an escaped slave who settled in Ohio. She grew up among the 'large, extended and complex Perry clan' in the small town of Yellow Springs, where she lives today. The Perrys, from her account, are a lively, idiosyncratic family of storytellers; and Perrys appear, under that very name, in some of her books. Her grandmother was reputed to be part Cherokee Indian, and she herself is the mother of an interracial family; these two elements of her

2. Virginia Hamilton, Newbery Award Acceptance, as above, pp. 129–36.
3. Helen Cresswell, author's note in *A Sense of Story* (Longman, 1971), first edition, p. 64.

background are worth remembering in connection with *Arilla Sun Down*. She has a deep sense of roots: of rootedness in a family which itself is rooted in a place. And the place is in America.

> What I am compelled to write can best be described as some essence of the dreams, lies, myths and disasters befallen a clan of my blood relatives whose troubled footfall is first discernible on this North American continent some one hundred fifty years ago. Some essence, then, of their language and feeling, which through space-time imagery I project as the unquenchable spirit of a whole people. The fact that others recognize my projections as reality simply reveals how similar is the spiritual struggle of one group to that of another. I claim the right (and an accompanying responsibility) by dint of genealogy to 'plumb the line' of soul and ancestry.[4]

Clearly Virginia Hamilton is concerned as a writer with the black, or non-white, experience. To the best of my recollection, no fictional character in any of her work up to the time of writing is white. But there is no taint of racism in her books; as she said herself in the article from which I have just quoted, 'the experience of a people must come to mean the experience of humankind'. All through her work runs an awareness of black history, and particularly of black history in America. And there is a difference in the furniture of her writing mind from that of most of her white contemporaries: dream, myth, legend and ancient story can be sensed again and again in the background of naturalistically-described present-day events.

Her first book, *Zeely* (1967), exemplifies this and other Hamilton qualities. Elizabeth, who is calling herself Geeder by way of make-believe while on holiday in the country, sees the beautiful, regal, immensely-tall Zeely first as a night-traveller (a phrase which of course connotes escape from slavery) and then, obsessively, as a Watutsi queen. At the end of the story, when for the first and only time she actually talks to Zeely, she faces

4. Virginia Hamilton, 'High John is Risen Again,' *Horn Book*, April 1975, reprinted in *Crosscurrents of Criticism,* ed. Heins (The Horn Book Inc., 1977), pp. 159–67.

the truth that Zeely is a very tall girl who looks after hogs. Zeely has accepted herself as what she is, and with the aid of a parable of seeking and finding she helps Geeder to do the same. She is not a queen; and perhaps there is an implication that for black Americans to look back towards supposed long-lost glories in Africa is unfruitful. Yet the story manages at the same time to hold within itself a different truth, almost a contradiction. There is a sense in which Geeder's illusions have not been illusions at all; in which the figure of Zeely does embody that of the night-traveller, who, according to Geeder's Uncle Ross, 'must be somebody who wants to walk tall . . . it is the free spirit in any of us breaking loose'; in which, as Geeder says at the end, Zeely truly is a queen as well as a hog-keeper. If there is a simple message here for younger children (and I do not think Virginia Hamilton would scorn to offer a simple message to young children) it can be summed up in those two words 'walk tall'; but it is a simplicity that has profound resonances.

The House of Dies Drear (1968), with its crowded action and melodramatic trappings, is in many ways at the opposite fictional pole from *Zeely*. Thomas is the eldest child of a black historian's family which moves into a great rambling old house, once a station on the Underground Railroad, supposedly-haunted home of a murdered abolitionist, and now guarded by 'that massive, black and bearded man some souls called Pluto'. Thomas and his father penetrate the labyrinthine complexities of the house, discovering at last the extraordinary treasure which is its ultimate secret; and they drive off those who have threatened it. Here is a tale of mystery and excitement; of all Miss Hamilton's novels it is the one with the most obvious attractions to the child reading for the story. Indeed, an adult reader may feel she has been rather too free with the Gothic embellishments.

   The house of Dies Drear loomed out of mist and murky sky, not only gray and formless, but huge and unnatural. It seemed to crouch on the side of a hill high above the highway. And it had a dark, isolated look about it that set it at odds with all that was living.

A Sounding of Storytellers

The hidden buttons, sliding panels and secret passages can too easily suggest a commercially-inspired Haunted House from a superior fairground: at the same time gruesome and giggly. And the play-acting with which 'our' side frightens off superstitious intruders at the end is not really worthy of this author. One has initial doubts, too, about the marvellously-preserved treasure cave of Dies Drear, with its magnificent tapestries, carpets, glassware, Indian craft work and so on. Is it appropriate to the story that there should be a tangible, financially-valuable treasure, and anyway is it the right kind of thing for a dedicated abolitionist to have and to hide?

Here however one must recall Virginia Hamilton's comment on the tendency of the people and properties in her books to turn into emblems. It is a reasonable supposition that the treasure represents a cultural inheritance, of which Mr Pluto is the guardian or some kind of guardian spirit. The whole book has a strong, almost tangible sense of the presence of the past. It is a dramatic and at the same time a rather rambling piece of work, with something in it of the character of the house itself: much of it is below the surface, passages open out of the story in all directions, some are explored and some are only glanced into. It is highly interesting, highly readable, but it does not quite succeed in being both an exciting adventure story and a satisfying work of art.

The mysteries of *The Planet of Junior Brown* (1971) are of a different order from those of *Dies Drear*: more akin to those of *Zeely* and of the later novels. *Junior Brown* is not fantasy, as the word is commonly understood: the laws of nature are never broken, and occasionally, as in the description of Junior's mother's asthmatic attack, there is an insistent, almost cruel realism. Yet there is much in the book that requires a different kind of assent from that which we give to an account of everyday events. The ex-teacher janitor who has a large rotating model of the solar system erected in the hidden basement room to which his truant friends come; the 'planets' of homeless boys dotted around the big city, each with its 'Tomorrow Billy' as leader; the lowering of 262-pound Junior Brown into the basement of a deserted building by means of a specially-rigged hoist: these carry a conviction which has more to do with the character and atmosphere of the story, the hypnotic power of the author to compel belief, than with literal probability.

Junior Brown, musically talented but imprisoned by the circumstances of his life, is befriended by Buddy, who is a loner of the streets, yet free. Junior is superficially much better off than Buddy: he has his home, his devoted mother, his music teacher, his talent. But his home is stifling; his mother is ill, all but deserted by her husband and disastrously possessive of Junior; his music teacher is deranged, he can't get at her piano, and his own at home has been castrated by removal of the strings, so that 'as Junior played on and on, the hammers rose and fell senselessly'.

Junior's fatness is one of the things that imprison him; it is also a hunger turned inside out. Buddy understands Junior's need. When Mr Pool the janitor is forced to dismantle his solar system and discontinue his refuge, when Junior – his mental state deteriorating – 'catches' his music teacher's delusion of having an ever-present unwanted relative, there is only one thing for it: to treat Junior as the lost boy he really is, and install him in the deserted-basement 'planet' where Buddy is Tomorrow Billy.

A planet in this story is a person's refuge, and perhaps also his sphere of action. There is an analogy between the huge uncaring city and the vast indifference of space by which planets are surrounded. The school from which Junior Brown and Buddy are alienated, but in which they find a temporary home in the janitor's room, expresses the same analogy on a smaller scale. Buddy, coping and compassionate, instinctual and imaginative, 'swinging wild and cool through city streets', is a forerunner, a leader into the future, a kind of saint of the streets. Too good to be true? Too good to be literally true, I think; it is hard to suppose that a homeless street lad could be so noble, so uncorrupted by hardship and by the company of those already corrupted. But when Buddy affirms on the last page that 'the highest law is for us to live for one another', he surely speaks not as Buddy Clark but as Tomorrow Billy, a mythological figure, conceivably related to the High John de Conquer who was the hero and inspiration of slaves in the last century.

M. C. Higgins the Great (1974) achieved the feat, so far unique, of winning the Newbery Medal, the National Book Award and the *Boston Globe-Horn Book* Award. M.C. is the early-teenage black boy who sits on that pole, which was his reward from his father for swimming the Ohio River, and which he has equipped with a bicycle saddle, pedals and a pair of wheels that enable him to move the pole in a slow, sweeping arc. The title 'the Great' is self-awarded, a joke, but by the time the book is read the reader is likely to feel it justified; for M.C. *is* great, he *does* ride high; though he is poor and presumably uneducated he has wisdom, competence, determination. At the end he is building a wall which he hopes will hold back the spoilheap that threatens his home; he will inherit and defend the family territory. Unlike Buddy Clark, though, he is not a saint or an inspirational figure; he is human, makes mistakes, has his inadequacies.

On the surface, not a great deal happens in this novel. The Higgins family lives on the mountain to which Great-grandmother Sarah came, unfree, with her child in her arms, long time ago. A travelling dude arrives with a tape recorder, and M.C. thinks, wrongly, that this means his mother will become a singing star and they will move away. A wandering girl also arrives, camps beside the lake, intrigues and disturbs M.C., but disappears without a good-bye. The other things that happen in the book are even less dramatic. But nothing is insignificant. Events in *M. C. Higgins the Great* either define the people and their situation or else, by apparently small redirections (like points on a rail track) change the courses of people's lives. The most important event happens inside M.C.: his acceptance of his own rootedness in Sarah's Mountain and his determination to stop that spoilheap.

Roots, more than anything else, are what this novel is about: roots in place and also the roots of ancestry. After telling M.C. how Great-grandmother Sarah came to the mountain, his father, Jones Higgins, sings some words from a song she used to sing. The words have been passed down through succeeding generations, but Jones doesn't know what they mean: 'I guess even Great-grandmother Sarah never knew. Just a piece of her language she remembered.' Both Jones and M.C. occasionally have a sense of the presence of Sarah on the mountain. Jones says:

'Times in the heat of the day. When you not thinking much on nothing. When you are resting quiet. Trees, dusty-still. You can hear Sarah a-laboring up the mountain, the baby whimpering. She says "Shhh! Shhh!" like a breeze. But no breeze, no movement. It's just only Sarah, as of old. . . She climbs eternal. Just to remind us that she hold claim to me and to you and each one of us on her mountain.'

M.C. in fact has semi-mystical dreams and visions which link him with his past, and has a lingering half-belief in spirits. Jones is frankly superstitious, and this is harmful in his refusal to have anything to do with the 'witchy', six-fingered but perfectly harmless Killburns. M.C. does not go along with that; he is wiser, and Ben Killburn is his friend, though he has to assure himself that Ben's extra fingers aren't 'wildly waving and making magic'. It may be noted that M.C.'s wisdom is itself rooted in the earth and does not move away from it; he is hopelessly naïve about the visiting dude and about Mama's prospects of stardom. Two more small but significant events may be noted at the very end of the story: Jones accepts, albeit reluctantly, the presence of Ben Killburn on his property, helping M.C. to build the wall, and he gives the boys a gravestone to build into it.

'See it,' M.C. said. 'It's Great-grandmother Sarah's.' The markings were worn but the name was still readable.
'Why did your father bring it?' Ben wanted to know.
'Because,' M.C. said. He thought a long moment, smoothing his hand over the stone. Finally he smiled. 'To make the wall strong.'

It is the reinforcement, once more, of the present by the past.
The Adams family in *Arilla Sun Down* are interracial. Arilla's

mother is a light-skinned black woman, beautiful, and a teacher of dancing. Her father is part-black, part American Indian; and her older brother Jack Sun Run, though neither more nor less Indian than Arilla, asserts himself to be 'a blood'. Arilla feels overshadowed; doesn't know who or what she is.

Jack Sun Run – handsome, flamboyant, a brilliant horseman – is the dominant figure in this novel; but he is a more subtly ambiguous creation than any in Virginia Hamilton's earlier books. There's a sense in which he is a phoney: 'playing the brave warrior', as his mother unkindly says, and, for instance, showing off shamelessly at Arilla's birthday party:

> He is dressed up in corduroys and a white shirt, with moccasins on his feet, old and soft, fitting like ballet slippers. A white felt band holding back his hair and with beadwork fashioned in the cloud design of the south-west Amerinds. . . It's the combination of moccasins, headband, shirt. My brother is gifted, and the girls know it and are caught.

Yet the phoney and the genuine are not entirely incompatible. There is something in Jack Sun Run's blood and background, and in his father's, that will come out and that will always be strange to Mother, who doesn't share it. And it is there in Arilla, too. In flashbacks to her earlier childhood, Arilla recalls half-forgotten experiences and encounters with the People: especially her friend, mentor, storyteller and source of wisdom, an old man called James False Face. Arilla receives – reluctantly, as a birthday present – a horse; she learns to ride well, and saves Jack Sun Run's life after an accident while out riding in fearful conditions. That is how she earns the name of Arilla Sun Down, becomes able to see Jack as human rather than as a being of sunlike power and brilliance, and also puts herself level with him, since he saved her life as a small child.

But in the end it is through her father that Arilla comes into a share of the Indian inheritance. Every year Dad, who is a supervisor in a college dining hall, disappears for a while, and Jack has to go and bring him back. Now, with Jack in hospital, the duty falls on Arilla. She finds Dad where he is known to be, up in the country of his people; and he has gone sledding – flying wild and free over the snow. Arilla sleds with him, as she did when a small child. Sledding, riding, even roller-skating: these are important, she needs the movement for the nomad that is in her. There is something of the experience, the transmitted wisdom of the People in her, too. All this is more real than the earlier posturings of Jack Sun Run.

Lastly there is the thing that is Arilla's own, the gift that is individually hers, that comes out in her urge to write. It goes with the name that old James has given her, along with his stories: her secret name. It is there in the book, at a key moment, a moment remembered by Arilla from years before. In this memory James has just died; Arilla is feverish and she seems to hear him speaking to her of life and death, and concluding:

'*Wordkeeper?*'

'*I hear you.*'

'*Remember who you are.*'

In its movement back and forth in time, and its shifts of style, *Arilla Sun Down* may make one think occasionally of the Faulkner of *The Sound and the Fury*. But it is an original work, and a poetic one. Among many memorable lyric passages are Arilla's childhood recollection of sledding with Father, and, in her 'present-day' narrative, a parallel pages-long account of roller-skating, both capturing to an astonishing degree the poetry of motion. There is another remarkable passage near the end, when Arilla has gone to collect Dad; they have been sledding, as they did long ago, and they are turning away when the moon comes up, clear and brilliant:

Dad pointed at it. All of a sudden his hand looked like it was lit. He turned back to the fence and pointed at the vastness out there. And threw back his head. Threw it back in a kind of heave.

And howled.

The sound of a great wolf circling out far into the night. With yip-yips of little cubs. And sounds of gentle wolves and fierce half-grown wolves, so eager. All to end with the call of the great father wolf, who had the deepest chest. Who was most alone and stalking. And was Dad.

The sound colliding with echoes of itself all around; then vanishing on the moonlight of the night. Again and again. Howling.

I knew better than to say a word. It was a sound so deep of my dad, it was like being sacred. And me given a privilege to hear. I knew how to keep my mouth closed.

For a long time we stood at the fence. I was freezing now, but I waited. Looking out into darkness you couldn't see through. Looking, not a word, until Dad took hold of the sled and started up the trail.

After this they go home, content.

It is possible to do violence to a book by intrusive probing; by partial or misleading explanation. If I have given some impression of the power and strangeness of *Arilla Sun Down,* and left anyone feeling the need to read or reread it, I have probably done what is most useful. It is a book that takes risks. It is not for casual, easy reading, and among young people (or adults) it is likely to be appreciated only by a minority, and perhaps fully understood by none. The read book is always a collaboration between writer and reader, and this one requires that the reader should willingly contribute his or her own imaginative effort. It offers in return the high delight of sharing in an achieved work of art.

Virginia Hamilton

Virginia Hamilton writes:

Some authors write particularly for young people because of the
wonderfully clear and sweet memories they keep from their own
childhoods, memories which they feel a strong need to share with
others. But like all authors, we write also because creating fiction is
what we care to do best of all. Each of us believes that he or she has a
way of putting words down that is unlike any other author's.

Much of my time is spent transforming the source – all that I am
able to comprehend from the living experience – into a coherent form
of the novel. Therefore, writing over a period of time tends to stand
for what living has meant to me. I constantly search for new ways to
express this essence of living that belongs solely to me. As my writing
changes and I hope grows, so must the language I use to express it.

It is my wish never to be bored writing nor to bore children reading
what I've written. This may be the reason why, over the last decade,
I've become less preoccupied with my own roots. Only so much can
be said concerning one's heritage, and surely five or so books on the
subject is quite enough. Not to say that at some time in the future I
won't return to themes of the dark experience. But when I do, it might
be from an entirely new vantage, perhaps from a view of the American
Civil War and approached from the direction of folk humour and
magic. There are huge amounts of comedy hidden within the black
experience, which isn't explored in books for the young.

Now, I find myself curious about survivors of all kinds. By definition, survivors are fit for survival. Some will survive the cataclysm
while most will perish. Is it chance or fate that the few survive, or do
they survive because of an inherent difference from the victims who
go under? Who are survivors? Are they you and I, or something we
hold within us, such as our grace, our courage or our luck? And could
they be our genes?

Genes certainly are within us. Perhaps *they* created us in body and
mind to be used just for themselves, with their preservation as the
ultimate rationale for *our* existence, as some scientists now believe.

Yet, that which our genes might do for their own survival may also benefit us.

L. Larison Cudmore writes in *The Center of Life*,[1] 'Among the at least 800,000 unused genes we have, there may be (the power of) flight, which seems to be the ultimate end of evolution. . . Flight is beloved and envied by almost every human being, and is an integral part of our myths, dreams and religions . . . The Icarus myths . . . may really be in our genes, not just the imagination of an ancient storyteller.'

Might not the human survivors of a cataclysm receive the revelation to flee the area hours, even years before the catastrophe? Was that most fabulous survivor of all time, old Noah, hearing messages from God or subconscious nudges from a distraught gene pool? Is it possible that telepathy, clairvoyance, the prophecy of the ancients, genius, might be a mutation of genes?

Thus, I'm at work on the *Justice* cycle of fantasies,[2] in which seemingly ordinary children have tapped new gene information which is accessible to them after thirty million years of dormancy. They have power which may prove dangerous in the present world but which is necessary, even vital for a future one. My assumption is that the gifted among us, even the strange and the eccentric, could be nature's way of preserving special abilities that the human race may need in a future world. Who's to say? It's an idea for wonder.

1. *The Center of Life* (Quadrangle, 1977).
2. *Justice and her Brothers* (Greenwillow, 1978); *Dustland; The Gathering* (still being written).

E. L. Konigsburg

Elaine Lobl Konigsburg was born in New York City in 1930 but spent most of her childhood in Pennsylvania. She studied chemistry at the Carnegie Institute of Technology and at the University of Pittsburgh and then taught for a while when she and her husband moved to Jacksonville, Florida, where they still live with their three children. Her first book, Jennifer, Hecate, Macbeth, William McKinley and Me, Elizabeth *was a Newbery Medal Honor Book for 1968, and her second,* From the Mixed-Up Files of Mrs Basil E. Frankweiler *won the Newbery Medal itself in the same year. Her subsequent books include* About the B'nai Bagels *(1969),* A Proud Taste for Scarlet and Miniver *(1973) and* Father's Arcane Daughter *(1976).*

As a postgraduate student of chemistry, Elaine Konigsburg had her adventures in the laboratory front line: 'a few minor explosions, burned hair, and stained and torn clothes'.[1] That was just a beginning. Subsequently she has taught in school, studied art and art history, travelled, brought up a family, made herself an expert on baseball, and of course become a distinguished writer and illustrator of children's books. And according to the back flap of *The Second Mrs. Giaconda* (1975) she has 'a small garden of wild things in Jacksonville, Florida'. It is hardly surprising that a person of such various talents should be fascinated by Leonardo da Vinci. Mrs Konigsburg seems almost indeed to have invited comparison with Leonardo in the closing sentences of a speech at Fresno, California, in 1975:

1. David Konigsburg, biographical note on E. L. Konigsburg, *Horn Book*, August 1968, reprinted in *Newbery and Caldecott Medal Books, 1966–1975* (The Horn Book Inc., 1975), pp. 42–4.

... writing for children demands a certain kind of excellence: the quality that Salai helped to give to Leonardo, the quality that young readers demand, as Renaissance viewers demanded it – that works of art must have weight and knowledge behind them, that works of art must have all the techniques and all the skills; they must never be sloppy but must never show the gears. Make it nonchalant, easy, light. The men of the Renaissance called that kind of excellence *sprezzatura*.

And because Salai appreciated this quality, Leonardo kept him with him. And because children demand it subliminally and appreciate it loudly, and because I do, too, I write for children.[2]

I do not think there is a Leonardo writing for the children's lists today; it would be astonishing if there were. But Mrs Konigsburg has certainly produced books which differ remarkably from each other, which display impressively different forms of expertise, and which, to tell the truth, are decidedly uneven (as were the works of the great master himself). If there were anyone in the field who could claim a fringe of the Leonardo mantle, it would be she.

She is endlessly inventive and ingenious, and she is not afraid of being clever. In her novels of contemporary life, her situations are apt to be extraordinary and her characters idiosyncratic. Even her titles call attention to themselves. Those of her first two books – *Jennifer, Hecate, Macbeth, William McKinley and Me, Elizabeth* (1967) and *From the Mixed-Up Files of Mrs. Basil E. Frankweiler* (1967) – are not only showy but also inconveniently long, and must be an irritation to anyone who has to catalogue them or ask for them in a bookshop. (In Britain the former was mercifully shortened to *Jennifer, Hecate, Macbeth and Me*.) After these, the title *(George)*(1970) can only be described as gimmicky, and its brackets must cause further confusions. The title of *The Second Mrs. Giaconda* is rather a tease, since the lady does not appear until the penultimate page. On the other hand, *A Proud Taste for Scarlet and Miniver* (1973) is surely a splendid, properly colourful and resounding title for a book about Eleanor of Aquitaine.

2. E. L. Konigsburg, 'Sprezzatura: a Kind of Excellence', *Horn Book*, June 1976.

E. L. Konigsburg

Mrs Konigsburg's own illustrations make a valuable contribution to her books. She lacks the fluency of line that suggests a natural draughtsman, but her sense of design is strong and she can convey character: look at Jennifer, or at Claudia and Mrs Frankweiler in *Mixed-Up Files*. And as her own artist she has the huge advantage of knowing exactly which passages the author would most like illustrated, and how the author thinks people and places should look.

She made a spectacularly sudden impression on the children's book scene with *Jennifer, Hecate etc.* and *Mixed-Up Files,* which both came out in the same year and which were respectively a Newbery honours-list book and the winner of the Newbery Medal itself. This swift recognition reflects credit on the Newbery–Caldecott committee, and is also in my view a correct assessment of the relative merits of the two books. *Jennifer, Hecate etc.* is original, amusing and full of promise; *Mixed-Up Files* is an outstandingly good book, a winner by any standard, and shows the promise rapidly fulfilled.

Elizabeth, the narrator of *Jennifer, Hecate etc.*, is a lonely new arrival in the fifth grade at William McKinley Elementary School (hence the *William McKinley and Me, Elizabeth* part of the title). Jennifer is the solitary child who confers friendship on Elizabeth, in a relationship in which she, Jennifer, is always the leader. The leadership indeed is formalized, for Jennifer claims to be a witch, 'a witch all the time and not just on Hallowe'en', and takes on Elizabeth as her apprentice. Jennifer is cool, self-possessed, imaginative, and for a child dignified; she doesn't take kindly to condescension from teacher or librarian. She gives little away, doesn't answer questions, doesn't invite Elizabeth home. She is a prodigious reader; and when Elizabeth asks her what she does besides read, she says, 'I think.'

Elizabeth has to obey rules for her apprenticeship, observe prohibitions, eat specified foods (and bring others, more palatable, to Jennifer); and such is Jennifer's seriousness and confidence that Elizabeth believes in the witchcraft, believes she is learning, and even appears to have some small successes at the party given by cute, detestable Cynthia. But although it is never stated, an adult reader may guess that Jennifer and Elizabeth, in the manner of children, both believe and disbelieve. When they start boiling up an ointment to enable them to fly, and reach the stage at which according to the recipe a live toad should be dropped into the brew, the point has been reached at which the game must stop. After a break, Jennifer and Elizabeth resume their relationship on a different footing, laughing and playing together in ordinary ways, just friends.

Everything that happens in this story is filtered through Elizabeth. Jennifer is never seen from the inside. But the story is about her, and about the two girls' relationship, at least as much as it is about the more ordinary Elizabeth. There is a great deal of subtlety in it, as well as humour and sympathy. A point about Jennifer which I have not previously mentioned, and which is barely referred to in the text although it is evident throughout from the pictures, is that Jennifer is black. The book is not concerned with blackness as an issue, and one might too easily assume that the author has merely 'integrated' her story. But it is not so. Make Jennifer white and the book ceases to work. She is the only black child at her school, and her pride, resourcefulness and self-sufficiency must be seen in that light. By force of character she has made something positive from being the odd one out. This achievement is never stated, only implied; and by pointing it out I risk making the author seem more heavy-footed than she is. Mrs Konigsburg steps so delicately over this potentially tricky ground that one hardly realizes she has been there at all.

Running away from home is one of the most familiar themes of children's fiction; but a cool, *organized* running away, as in *Mixed-Up Files*, is surely original. Claudia Kincaid thinks herself hard-done-by as the oldest child of four and the only girl, but from the beginning she intends to come back when everyone has learned a lesson in Claudia-appreciation. And we see from the start what sort of person Claudia is: she doesn't like discomfort; she is not just running *from* somewhere, she is running *to* somewhere. She wants to find 'a large place, a comfortable place, an indoor place, and preferably a beautiful place'. And she knows she can't do it without money. 'Living in the suburbs had taught her that everything costs.' So Claudia makes her plans carefully; she decides on the Metropolitan Museum of Art in New York, and she will take with her the second of her three brothers, Jamie, who already shows alarming signs of financial wizardry. (He has accumulated the enormous fortune, by small-boy standards, of twenty-four dollars and forty-three cents, largely through being suspiciously successful at cards.)

It is all dazzlingly ingenious. The details of the operation are both intriguing and plausible. One watches with something like awe as Claudia and Jamie successfully install themselves in the museum, discover how to dodge the staff and guards, and find themselves a magnificent bed and an equally magnificent bath (in the fountain, with an income from wishing-pennies and nickels thrown in). The older-sister-with-younger-brother relationship has just the right balance, and the conversations of Claudia and Jamie have a remarkably authentic air, considering the improbability of the circumstances. Claudia herself is a wholly admirable creation: cool, self-possessed and somewhat formidable, a child with obvious and interesting potentiality for growth.

And Claudia wants to come back different as a result of her experience. One might think that the adventure itself would be sufficient; it is unique and individual enough. But as she remarks at the end, it was all planned by the usual careful Claudia, and it became 'like living at home away from home'. So she begins a new quest: to find out the truth about a statue of an angel, acquired by the museum for $225 and possibly the work of Michelangelo. Their inquiries take the children to the home of rich, elderly Mrs Basil E. Frankweiler, who sold the statue to the museum. And Mrs Frankweiler, realizing Claudia's need to make a significant discovery, allows her to find 'a very special, very old piece of paper' which contains the clue. Yes, the figure was really Michelangelo's; yes, there on the old piece of paper is a sketch that shows how the idea came from his head to his hand. Claudia is entranced, fulfilled. Mrs Frankweiler, who tells the story, sums it up:

'Claudia doesn't want adventure. She likes baths and feeling comfortable too much for that sort of thing. Secrets are the kind of adventure she needs. Secrets are safe, and they do much to make you different. On the inside where it counts.'

The narrative takes the form of an account of the matter supplied by Mrs Frankweiler to her lawyer Saxonberg. This seems a curious device, since Mrs Frankweiler herself does not appear on the scene until almost the end, and she has to be made aware of the thoughts and feelings of Claudia and sometimes Jamie throughout the whole experience, as well as a great many small details and precisely-recalled conversations. Presumably the purpose is to allow the author to offer some adult insights, such as the remarks of Mrs Frankweiler quoted above. I do not think the device is altogether effective; there is some clumsiness about it and some loss of conviction, especially at those points, scattered through the story, when the reader is 'with' Claudia and Jamie but is suddenly reminded that the narrator is Mrs Frankweiler. There is however a particular and pleasing subtlety that could easily escape notice. It is the bond across the generations which is formed between Claudia and Mrs Frankweiler. They are the same kind of person; Mrs Frankweiler might well be a Claudia grown old.

It may be noted that the children's parents never appear. This omission is obviously not accidental. The disappearance of two children for several days would be a fearful experience for parents; to introduce them would be to make some degree of identification with them by the reader inevitable, and would give a different shape and feeling to the story. Since the narrative is concerned with the positive side of the adventure of Claudia and Jamie, it is as well to keep parental agony out of it (though there are a few slight references which prevent any feeling of callousness). I do not see this as a fault. It seems a wholly unnecessary use of coincidence, however, when Mrs Frankweiler's lawyer turns out to be the children's grandfather – a fact that does not have any relevance to the way the action develops – and there is an unconvincing narrative-within-a-narrative when Mrs Frankweiler incorporates a report from her chauffeur on the children's conversation in the back of her Rolls Royce as he is driving them home after their escapade. *Mixed-Up Files* is by no means a flawless book, but it is a very good one, and up to the time of writing I am inclined to think that Mrs Konigsburg, though her work is continually interesting, has not improved on it.

About the B'nai Bagels (1969) has not been published in England – a fact which I do not find surprising, since much of it is hard to follow without an understanding of baseball. It is a pity all the same that this difficulty deprives British children of an intriguing picture of Jewish suburban family life. The 'B'nai Bagels' is the nickname of the Little League team of the B'nai Brith; and Mark Setzer has a problem when his mother becomes the team manager. Management by Mother is not all he has to contend with: there's the strain of his coming Bar Mitzvah, the ceremony at which he will become a man and can participate as an adult in religious services; and there's the apparent loss of his best friend. The main theme presumably is that of growing-up and of discovering that 'you don't become a man overnight'; sub-themes have to do with the overlap of public and private capacities – seen in the small but vivid context of a junior sports team – and with the need of young people for some privacy in their lives.

None of these themes, it will be noticed, is specifically Jewish. *About the B'nai Bagels* has been criticized by a Jewish observer, along with other books, for 'failure to deal with the real problems of Jewish life';[3] but surely it is not trying to do anything so ambitious, and it is not under obligation to do so. Mrs Konigsburg has chosen to write about a comfortably-off Jewish family who are not suffering discrimination or carrying any chips on their shoulders; and if, as the same commentator complains, they are slack and garbled in their religious observances, it is no doubt regrettable but it is not incredible.

3. Eric A. Kimmel, 'Jewish Identity in Juvenile Fiction: a Look at Three Recommended Books', *Horn Book*, April 1973, reprinted in *Crosscurrents of Criticism*, ed. Heins (The Horn Book Inc., 1977), pp. 150–58.

The most notable person in the book is team-manager Mother, with her salty conversation and her habit of appealing to her Maker, who appears to live somewhere around the light fixture on the kitchen ceiling. 'When I think of all the hours of stuffed cabbage I put into that boy,' she tells Him, complaining of the taste in food of her elder son. 'Wasted, just wasted.' *About the B'nai Bagels* is dedicated to 'my own dear mother, who knows nothing about baseball but almost everything about love and stuffed cabbage'. Its celebration of that well-known figure the Jewish momma, in a likeable if somewhat stereotyped form, is one of the pleasant features of an attractive and funny, though not very important, book.

With (*George*) Mrs Konigsburg introduced a new theme which she was to repeat later with variations: that of the *alter ego*, the inner self or perhaps (as in *The Second Mrs. Giaconda*) the complementary outside person who supplies what is missing to complete the personality of an individual. Ben, aged twelve, is brilliant at science and works alongside the seniors; George is a little man who lives inside Ben, his 'concentric twin'. Hence the brackets around his name. George is imaginative and refreshingly cynical, whereas Ben is apt to conform and to seek out conventional objectives. George is thus a metaphor for some part of the complex psychological structure of Ben; he has counterparts in literature and everyday figure-of-speech, and even in writings on psychology. But George is a metaphor with a speaking voice, and makes irreverent comments on the doings of Ben and others; in fictional terms he is a separate character.

Ben would like to work with William, a senior; but William is now doing a research project with Cheryl, a girl of his own age. Their teacher is Mr Berkowitz, who meets and becomes fond of Ben's divorced mother. Laboratory equipment is stolen, and suspicion falls on Ben, whose dialogues with George lead to his being sent for psychiatric treatment. When Ben discovers that William and Cheryl have the stolen equipment and are using it to make the drug L.S.D., he and George decide magnanimously to take the blame, in order to keep the school and

E. L. Konigsburg

Mr Berkowitz out of trouble. Ben can get away with a false confession, being 'young and not normal'.

There is something about this whole story that makes one a little uneasy, and its outcome seems dubious at more than one level. There is first the simple question of probability: could a child of twelve take the blame for so serious a business in total independence of the adult world – and would the adult world believe him? And is it ethically an acceptable solution? We are told that Ben's mother does not lose custody of him, as she well might, and that William and Cheryl are punished by getting failing grades for the year . . . but would not the probable and morally proper outcome be that Ben should tell the truth and let the consequences follow?

One is left, finally, in doubt about the acceptability of George at all. As pure fantasy or as a conscious figment of Ben's imagination he would be all right; but when he is the cause of Ben's undergoing psychiatric treatment, when he is there at the end telling Ben to 'listen to me always. . . If you don't shut me up forever now, I'll be rich within you. You'll always have me to fall back on,' one must feel one is leaving Ben in a deeply ambiguous mental state. Surely there is a danger that some children may be troubled and confused, consciously or unconsciously, by this book. And even if one assumes that nobody will actually take any harm from it, I think one must nevertheless say that (*George*) is pretentious; that, as with the title itself, there is something gimmicky in the concept of the 'concentric twins'. When George says disapprovingly of William and Cheryl that they work hard at being different, one feels that, at this stage in her career, the same might have been said of Mrs Konigsburg herself.

Of Mrs Konigsburg's remaining stories of contemporary life, the four brief tales which make up *Altogether, One at a Time* (1971) seem to me to be more satisfying than the later full-length novels. All four could be called, in James Joyce's sense of the word, epiphanies: sudden insights into human nature and relationships, brief flashes of illumination on some aspect of the endless subject of what life is about. Stanley and the boys at his party in *Inviting Jason*; Lewis and his would-be-young grand-mother in *The Night of the Leonids*; Clara and the ghostly Miss Natasha in *Camp Fat*; above all, Momma, her blackness and her talent in *Momma at the Pearly Gates*: all are easily readable and one or two may appear slight, but there is more to them than meets the casual eye; they plant small time-bombs in the con-sciousness, perhaps to explode later. They are in fact very good short stories.

I can find little to say in favour of *The Dragon in the Ghetto Caper* (1974), a novel about a boy who is always drawing dragons – portentously symbolic – and whose friendship with a young married woman and visits to a black ghetto are neither convincing nor particularly interesting. *Father's Arcane Daughter* (1976) is much better, though still not E. L. Konigsburg at her best. A woman turns up at the home of Winston Carmichael and his handicapped sister Heidi, children of a rich Pittsburgh industrialist, and claims to be Caroline, their father's daughter by a former marriage. Caroline had been kidnapped seventeen years before, and was thought dead. Is the new Caroline genuine or an impostor? Can she pass the tests of memory and recognition? There is mystery and suspense here, and a thoughtful development of the story; for there comes a time when it no longer matters all that much whether the new Caroline is the real one or not. She fulfils the role of elder sister, puts physically-handicapped Heidi on the way to making use of her high intelligence, frees Winston from a burden of responsi-bility and guilt: that is her reality. There are the makings here of a very good novel, but it has not quite come together, and it is interesting to ask why. A minor reason, I think, is that Mrs Konigsburg, ingenious as always, makes recurrent use of a liter-ary device which in this case is intrusive and rather pointless; the prefacing of her chapters with snatches of dialogue from years afterwards which do not actually add to the story and merely constitute a series of puzzling and irritating hitches. The major reason, which is serious, is that she does not seem able to handle – or at any rate keeps away from – the strong emotions which this story ought to involve. Looking back, one can see that this

E. L. Konigsburg

is characteristic of her work; she is interested in ideas and issues, has humour and a sharp eye for personality, but she does not get deeply involved. It is just as well that Claudia in *Mixed-Up Files* is so cool and that the parents from whom she has run away are left out of the story.

Mrs Konigsburg's two historical novels feature famous and colourful personalities; they have bright surfaces but a similar lack of emotional depth. *A Proud Taste for Scarlet and Miniver* is successful all the same in its own way. It covers the adult life of Eleanor of Aquitaine, flamboyant and decisive, wife successively of the Kings of France and England. Once again there is an ingenious literary device. Eleanor is in heaven, waiting for her second husband, Henry II of England, to come Up after expiating his misdeeds; and her story is told in successive instalments by three of her contemporaries and finally herself. It is vivid, witty, full of epigram and paradox, and it is a view of history from the top: kings, nobles, castles, alliances, marriage bargains, betrayals, battles. The dialogue and the attitudes expressed are those of our own time; the narrators are all clever and articulate and have similar tones of voice. One is reminded at times of Bernard Shaw's *St. Joan*; at other times of the brilliance and clarity, yet flatness, which we associate with much of medieval art. Mrs Konigsburg's illustrations, suggestive of illuminated manuscript, aid the latter illusion. And there is some sheer fun, especially at the very end, when Henry II floats up to heaven accompanied by a gaunt bearded man and a squat one.

Henry took his first look at Eleanor in eight hundred years. He looked her over from toe to brow. Then he spoke, 'Good grief, madam! One of these men says that he is a Mr. Winston Churchill and that he governed England. How can a common man govern?'

'This one did quite well, actually,' Eleanor replied.

'You mean that a common man now sits on the throne of England?'

'No, Henry. A rather plain housewife does.'

'And this one,' Henry said, pointing to the tall man with the beard, 'says that he is a Mr. Abraham Lincoln and that he is an American lawyer and president. What is a president? And what in Heaven's name is an American?'

A Sounding of Storytellers

A Proud Taste for Scarlet and Miniver is a *tour de force*. Alone, I think, among Mrs Konigsburg's later books it is as good in its way as her first two. *The Second Mrs. Giaconda* unfortunately does not match it. The author has tried to answer the question why Leonardo da Vinci painted the second wife of an obscure Florentine merchant when the greatest people in Italy were trying in vain to get him to paint their portraits. The reason she gives is the speculative one that he was persuaded by his assistant Giacomo Salai. This however raises the equally difficult question: why did Leonardo retain for so many years the services of the dishonest and untalented Salai? Salai, who was of course an actual person, is at the heart of Mrs Konigsburg's book. By her account, he provided the wild element which the controlled Leonardo needed in order that his work should be great art.

This thesis, which cannot be proved or disproved, does not seem a particularly likely one, and Salai is an unattractive central character. The author is handicapped, too, in that she clearly felt unable in a children's book to draw attention to the near-certainty that Leonardo and Salai had a homosexual relationship. Altogether this is a flimsy and unconvincing piece of writing; and its worst deficiency is a total failure to convey the greatness of Leonardo. This admittedly is always difficult: to put the very great into fiction is a perilous undertaking. Readers will get an infinitely stronger sense of what Leonardo was by looking at that profound and mysterious self-portrait – fortunately reproduced in the book along with several of his works – than by reading Mrs Konigsburg's text.

Probably it is not an unmixed blessing to win the Newbery Medal at the outset of one's career. It gives a new writer a great deal to live up to. Elaine Konigsburg's subsequent work has been patchy and a little disappointing. But she is able, audacious, witty and full of ideas; and she is intelligent enough to learn from her mistakes. All being well, she has plenty of writing time ahead of her, and she must surely still have a great deal to contribute to children's literature.

E. L. Konigsburg

E. L. Konigsburg has written of the origins of her Newbery Medal-winning book *From the Mixed-up Files of Mrs. Basil E. Frankweiler*:

The idea for this book came from three experiences; two of them were reading experiences.

I read in the *New York Times* that the Metropolitan Museum of Art in New York City had bought a statue for $225. At the time of the purchase they did not know who had sculptured it, but they suspected that it had been done by someone famous in the Italian Renaissance; they knew that they had an enormous bargain. (The statue, by the way, is called The Lady with the Primroses; it is not an angel, and it was not sculptured by Michelangelo.)

Shortly after that article appeared in the paper I read a book that told the adventures of some children who upon being sent by ship from their island home to England are captured by pirates. In the company of the pirates, the children became piratical themselves; they lost the thin veneer of civilization that they had acquired in their island home.

The third thing that happened was a picnic that our family took while we were vacationing at Yellowstone Park. After buying salami and bread and chocolate milk and paper cups and paper plates and paper napkins and potato chips and pickles, we looked for a place to eat. There were no outdoor tables and chairs, so when we came to a clearing in the woods, I suggested that we all eat there. We all crouched slightly above the ground and began to spread out our meal. Then the complaints began: the chocolate milk was getting warm, and there were ants over everything, and the sun was melting the icing on the cupcakes. This was hardly having to rough it, and yet my small group could think of nothing but the discomfort.

I thought to myself that if my children ever left home, they would never become barbarians even if they were captured by pirates. Civilization was not a veneer to them; it was a crust. They would want at least all the comforts of home plus a few dashes of extra elegance. Where, I wondered, would they ever consider running to if they ever left home? They certainly would never consider any place less elegant than the Metropolitan Museum of Art.

Yes, the Metropolitan Museum of Art. All those magnificent beds and all that elegance. And then, I thought, while they were there, perhaps they would discover the secret of a mysterious bargain statue and in doing so, perhaps they could discover a much more important secret, the need to be different – on the inside where it counts.

Penelope Lively

Penelope Lively was born in Cairo, Egypt, in 1933, but settled in England after the war. She was educated at St Anne's College, Oxford, and later married a don. She began to write when her two children no longer needed her full-time attention and she is now the author of two novels for adults as well as several books for children. These include Astercote *(1970),* The Ghost of Thomas Kempe *(1973), which won the Carnegie medal,* The House in Norham Gardens *(1974), and* A Stitch in Time *(1976), for which she received a Whitbread Literary Award. Penelope Lively and her family now live in a village in Oxfordshire.*

In 1976 Penelope Lively published an introduction to the history of landscape under the title *The Presence of the Past* (1976). That title indicates the preoccupation underlying almost all her fiction for children, as well as her adult novel *The Road to Lichfield*.[1] She is not a historical novelist; her books are primarily about present-day people in present-day surroundings. But she is concerned with continuity: concerned to show that people and places as they are now incorporate the past, and that to see them without this dimension would be to see them 'flat', lacking perspective.

Mrs Lively's perspectives can be long ones, and she can work on more than one time-scale at once. Her award-winning children's book *A Stitch in Time* (1976) illustrates this characteristic. The events in the foreground of this story are those which take place during the brief period in which a girl called Maria is on holiday at Lyme Regis. Behind them lies Maria's personal history as the diffident only child of quiet, reserved parents. But

1. *The Road to Lichfield* (Heinemann, 1977).

the present for Maria is also affected by her imaginative involvement with a little girl called Harriet who lived in the same house more than a century before and who failed to finish her sampler. And Maria becomes fascinated by the fossils she finds in the blue lias of the cliffs and which she goes to see, in vastly greater variety, in the local museum: the creatures from 'forty million years ago, a hundred and eighty million, four hundred million', all of which have 'stepped out of the rock of which the place is made, the bones of it, those blue cliffs with which England ends'. There are, one might say, three orders of time past. There is the immediate past of living memory. Behind that is the historical past, extending over a few hundred or at the outside a few thousand years; and behind that again lie the immensities of prehistory, reaching back through spans of time that defeat the imagination. Events on all three time-scales have gone into the making of people and places as they are today: especially, in *A Stitch in Time* and Mrs Lively's other books, the people and landscape of England, for which she has deep feeling.

Penelope Lively sees a sense of continuity as essential to the life of the imagination. In an article in the *Horn Book* for August 1973, she regretted that modern children were in danger of losing the personal memory that came from contact with the old ('the grandmother at the fireside'), and suggested that 'it may be that books attending to memory, both historical and personal, are more important to children than ever before'. And in a passage that implies a degree of didactic intention, she went on to say:

Children need to sense that we live in a permanent world that reaches away behind and ahead of us, and that the span of a lifetime is something to be wondered at and thought about, and that – above all – people evolve during their own lives. People are never complete, as it were, but knowledge expands and contracts, opinions harden and soften, and people end up as a curious, irrational blend of experience and memory. Children have to be told about these things because they haven't had time to see how time works on them, or to see how it works on other people. They haven't yet seen the process, as we have

126

seen it on the faces of friends and relatives. They can't yet place themselves in a wider framework of time and space than *today* and *here*. But they have to, if they are not to grow up enclosed in their own personalities. Perhaps books can help, just a little.[2]

There must always, I think, be an element of rationalization in a writer's discussion of his or her own work; a book is there and its author, like anyone else, is interested and looks for explanations. The real ones may not be obvious. But when Penelope Lively writes of the importance of memory, of the continued life of the past in the present, there can be no doubt that she is talking about the sources of her inspiration, as well as about what she seeks to offer to children. Places stimulate her, and as she says in the article already referred to, 'certain places are possessed of a historical charge that sets the imagination flaring'.

In her early books, this historical 'charge' is very evident, and strikes one as being not only the inspiration but the motive force throughout; the concern with the personal evolution of the individual is not yet developed very far. Astercote, in the book of that title, published in 1970, is based on Hampton Gay, an Oxfordshire village which died in the Black Death. The Whispering Knights who give their name to Mrs Lively's second book (1971) are the Rollright Stones, on the border between Oxfordshire and Warwickshire; the stretch of road which features in *The Driftway* (1972) is now 'a perfectly ordinary road, B4525 from Banbury to Northampton', but is very ancient and was once a drovers' road along which herds were driven from Wales for sale in southern England. *The Wild Hunt of Hagworthy* (1971) is also firmly rooted in a place – West Somerset – but this story was probably inspired even more by what the author has called 'the widespread, ancient and powerful legend of the ghostly hunt'.

None of these books, to my mind, quite reaches the front

2. Penelope Lively, 'Children and Memory', *Horn Book*, August 1973, reprinted in *Crosscurrents of Criticism*, ed. Heins (The Horn Book Inc., 1975), pp. 226–33.

rank of recent children's fiction. The story of *Astercote* hinges on the disappearance of a chalice – saved from the ruined church of the lost village – which people in the surviving village near by think keeps the plague from coming back. When the chalice's disappearance is followed by a case of mumps, with symptoms similar to the early signs of plague, there is a panic which turns into ugly xenophobia. It is an interesting idea, but the development is curiously oblique; the fear of the returning plague soon ceases to be the villagers' motivation, and when they plan to barricade themselves against strangers we learn that 'nobody once mentioned the chalice, or the Black Death, or any of that. It was as though they'd forgotten what it had all been about in the first place.' The author seems to have lacked confidence in her own idea, and partly as a result of this the book fails to establish its probabilities and carry the reader across the unlikelihood of the story. Peter and Mair, the children from whose viewpoint events are seen, are just such a brother and sister as might appear in any standard adventure story, and the outcome – they recover the chalice from the young motor-biking hoodlum who'd stolen it, and all is well – is commonplace and anticlimactic.

Nevertheless, given that it was a first book and bore marks of being prentice work, *Astercote* looked very promising. Its successor, *The Whispering Knights*, was a disappointment. Martha, William and Susie concoct a witches' brew (*Macbeth* recipe, with modifications) and raise the malevolent spirit of Morgan le Fay, who represents 'the bad side of things' and is always turning up in various places and guises. It's the familiar running battle of Light against Dark; and the Dark of course is defeated, at least for the time being, with the aid of those mysterious stones and of the white witch Miss Hepplewhite. This, to be frank, is a bad book, parts of which read almost like a parody of early Garner. *The Wild Hunt of Hagworthy*, which came out in the same year, was quite strikingly better. In a Somerset village, the Vicar's idea of reviving the Horn Dance as a tourist attraction at the annual fête has implications that he is unaware of. The dance goes back to older beliefs than Christianity; it is really a hunt; it seeks an odd-person-out as its victim and has dehumanizing effects on its participants; and behind it lies the Wild Hunt of legend, which the Horn Dance may start up again by mimetic magic.

Lucy is a girl staying in the village; Kester, the bright but socially isolated boy with whom she forms a friendship, is identified, and identifies himself, as the victim of the hunt, driven into playing this role by something beyond his control. The menace grows steadily along the way to a powerful climax, and for the first time in Penelope Lively's work the human relationships are interesting. And her sense of landscape is beautifully worked into her account of Lucy's and Kester's friendship.

They walked in the woods, waist deep in bracken and the spires of willowherb, with the sunlight spitting and crackling through the roof of leaves far above their heads. They put sandwiches in haversacks and went for day-long expeditions, up over the Brendons and along the straight, bleak road across the top, with the distant glimpses of Devon flashing at them through gateways, through Dunster Park by Timberscombe to Wootton Courtney; up over silent stretches of moor and down through dark combes full of rushing water and dappled light.

Trees gave them shelter from the wind and the burning sun, they drank from streams that came down from the moor and rested on beds of bracken like the deer. They forgot the time, and knew only by the quality of the light glowing on trees and grass when it was evening. They lost themselves, and learned to distinguish landmarks in the rise and fall of the hills, the shape of the fields, the distribution of trees. Lucy quarried in the hedgerows for wild flowers, and made Kester list the names for her. They watched birds, traced a badger's path from his sett under a hedge, talked, slept, ate and talked again.

The Driftway is another book built on an attractive notion: an ancient road along which significant incidents from the past still linger. Sometimes in everybody's life, says the old man who gives Paul and Sandra a lift in his cart,

there's a time when a whole lot of living gets crammed into a few minutes, or an hour or two, and it may be good or bad, but it's brighter and sharper than all the rest put together. And it may be so sharp it can leave a shadow on a place – if the place is a special place – and at the right time other people can pick up that shadow. Like a message, see?

Paul picks up a series of such messages on a momentous, tormented day of his own life. But the story does not quite jell. Curiously, the effectiveness of the realistic opening – Paul hating his stepmother, dropping something into his pocket while preoccupied in the big store, and running away from trouble with his small sister in tow – works against the rest of the book. One wants badly to know what is going to happen to Paul and Sandra; and the incidents from the past that lie along the Driftway are not gripping enough to appear as other than traffic holdups in the progress of the story. And one doesn't quite believe in kind, informative old Bill, who comes along so providentially in his cart and understands so much, or in the way the experience so neatly and edifyingly unties the knots of Paul's hatred.

When these four books (of which the best, to my mind, is *The Wild Hunt of Hagworthy*) had appeared, it could have been said that Penelope Lively's talent was undoubted but did not seem outstanding in a field which had grown much more crowded over the preceding decade. The book that made her name was the next one, *The Ghost of Thomas Kempe* (1973), winner of the Carnegie Medal. This is a blessedly funny book, and infinitely welcome, since in children's as in adult fiction the gap for comedy of quality is always open. Thomas Kempe is an apothecary from the reign of King James I who has re-emerged in our own day as a poltergeist, after being bottled up in a wall in an ancient house. Like other poltergeists he is heard but not seen; but he can write. He leaves notices around in a crabbed, antique hand, advertising his services in sorcerie, astrologie, alchemie and physique, and he wants to make the small hero, James Harrison, aged ten, his apprentice. James, who reminds one a little of Tom Sawyer but rather more of Richmal Crompton's William, gets the blame for Thomas Kempe's activities. He asks his parents:

Penelope Lively

'What would you say if a house suddenly began to behave in a very peculiar way. If things kind of moved without anyone moving them and got mysteriously broken and books flew off bookshelves and bedcovers jumped off beds and doors banged themselves. That kind of thing?'

'I'd say there was a boy around,' said Mrs Harrison crisply. 'Aged ten or so.'

This is bad enough, but it soon becomes clear that Thomas Kempe is an unpleasant character: self-important, opinionated, malevolent. When he starts chalking libellous graffiti on walls and doors, it's too much, and James has to consult Bert Ellison, builder, decorator and part-time exorcist. He tells Bert there's a ghost in the house. 'Bert poured himself another cup of tea, and began to roll a cigarette. He stuck it in the corner of his mouth, lit it, and said, "Just the one?"' But not even Bert can get rid of Thomas Kempe until he grows weary of modern ways and in the end seeks help in finding his resting-place. Besides the humour of the story there is a pleasant, relaxed exploration of Mrs Lively's usual themes of time, memory, continuity; and an additional time-scale is introduced by James's discovery of the diary of a Victorian spinster lady whose nephew Arnold was staying with her when Thomas Kempe made a previous return to life. The nephew, appearing in the diary as a small boy who would have been a kindred spirit to James, is remembered by an old lady living nearby as a dignified elderly gentleman who visited the village school during her childhood: a detail which links the past with living memory and recalls Penelope Lively's remark, previously quoted, that 'the span of a lifetime is something to be wondered at and thought about'.

The title of *The House in Norham Gardens* (1974) correctly identifies the true centre of the story, even though the plot has its origins far away and long ago in New Guinea, and though each chapter opens with a passage describing the way of life of a New Guinea tribe in the last years before the twentieth century overtakes it. Clare, aged fourteen, lives with her ancient great-aunts in their huge, ugly Victorian house in North Oxford. The house belonged, years ago, to her anthropologist great-

131

grandfather; and in the attic is a shield painted with strange patterns, which he brought back from New Guinea, not realizing its magical significance to the tribesmen. Clare, in what seem to be dreams, becomes aware of brown men who desperately want it back; but in a final dream or vision which she has in hospital after a road accident she takes it back to them and they don't want it any more. They don't understand or even recognize it. The time has passed.

Though in a sense this is the matter of the story, the setting is Oxford, not New Guinea, and the main substance of the book is located away from the storyline. Once again this is a book about time and memory and continuity, about the four-dimensional wholeness of life, about the sadness yet inevitability of change; yet above all, and most simply, it is about the rambling impossible old house and the people who live in it. The affection between Clare and the aged academic aunts, feeble of body yet sharp and clear of mind, is beautifully and sensitively drawn. This is a novel of great human warmth, written with the calm authority of an author who by now is fully in command of her style and material.

Going Back (1975) is an evocation of wartime childhood in a country house in Somerset, as remembered by the grown woman who goes back to look at the place many years afterwards. Disciplinarian Father, to the general relief, is away at the war, and the house and grounds – which the children love, though he doesn't – are in the easygoing care of the tiny remaining staff. It's a happy life in the main, until Father insists on sending sensitive brother Edward away to boarding school; and the distancing through memory is performed with admirable skill, so that some events are recalled in clear bright detail, others through shifting mists, while some are totally lost. As in life, there are beginnings and endings, apparently random, sometimes poignant. Mike, the conscientious objector doing farm work, is a great friend of the children, and when at the end the prospect of Edward's imminent return to school drives them to run away, it is Mike whom they seek and find at the farm he has moved to, several miles away. Mike does what has to be done, and they last glimpse him on that very day, at the farm gate, waving good-bye. 'We never saw him again,' says the narrator. 'And I do not know what became of him.'

To a grown-up reader, *Going Back* is a pleasing and satisfying book; but it is about childhood as recalled in adult life, and it is arguable that its proper place is on the adult list, alongside *The Road to Lichfield*. This latter book cannot be discussed in the limited space of the present essay, but a few points of difference from the children's books may be briefly mentioned, and may be of interest since the underlying concern with past and present is in many ways similar. An obvious one is the adult viewpoint, the absence of a young eye at the centre; another is the inclusion of sexual and other material which is likely to be outside most children's range of knowledge and interest. A third is the introduction of a rather sophisticated concept which does not, I think, appear in any of Mrs Lively's children's books: the concept of the past as something that has a shifting nature in relation to the present. It doesn't stay put; and when narrator Anne finds that her dying father's life included a major area that she knew nothing about, the landscape of her own life is subtly changed. A fourth, and for the present purpose the last, difference is one that I cannot help seeing as a restriction on the adult novel. In the essay already quoted, Penelope Lively remarked that 'if a novel for adults concerns itself with memory, it will probably consider it in the context of a lifetime rather than in the context of history'; and this indeed *The Road to Lichfield* does. But as a result the writer has given herself far less imaginative scope than she had in, say, *The Driftway* or *A Stitch in Time*. The children's books are at an advantage in the size of the territory they can open up.

Mrs Lively has also written three stories, of short book length, for young children of perhaps seven or eight to ten. The most pleasing of these is *Fanny's Sister* (1977), which has a Victorian setting. Fanny prays to God for cherry tart and clotted cream for dinner; she also requests Him to take back the new baby she hadn't asked for. And when cherry tart and clotted cream are duly brought to the table the dreadful fear sweeps

Fanny that the Almighty might well intend to answer her other prayer as well. She runs away. That is not a new idea in children's fiction, but the events that follow are both unexpected and intriguing. It all adds up to an engaging and happily-concluded story which comes well within a youngish child's comprehension.

Penelope Lively's most recent book for children, at the time of writing, is *The Voyage of QV 66* (1978), a humorous story in a totally different vein from her previous work. There's been another Flood, and all the people (it seems) have been evacuated to Mars, leaving only animals behind. The crew of QV 66, a flat-bottomed boat, PROPERTY OF THE PORT OF LONDON AUTHORITY RETURN TO DEPOT 3, consists of Ned, a horse; Freda, a cow; Pal, a dog, the narrator (he can read, and he knows his name because he saw it with a picture of himself on a dog-food tin); Pansy, a kitten; Offa, a pigeon; and Stanley. Stanley has hands and feet, and although pictures of people give him the shivers he feels 'kind of connected to them'. Nobody's seen an animal like Stanley before, and the purpose of the voyage is to get to the London Zoo and find out what he is. He's the brains of the outfit, and he's also the one with imagination.

He tells stories about how when the sun goes down at night it turns into a golden fish and swims about, and that's why you must never go into the water at night or you might make it angry and it won't come up again in the morning. He tells stories about how the stars sing and how you can catch the wind if you run fast enough, and he says there are animals who live in the clouds. Look, he says, you can see the shapes of them. Freda says, 'That's not true, Stanley. You're making that up, aren't you?' And Stanley looks at her and says 'I don't know. P'raps I am and p'raps I'm not.'

Stanley – vain, excitable, clever, silly, endlessly curious – is the central figure of the story. He is of course a monkey (and a person), and alone among the animals he is fully characterized; the rest are drawn with a few broad strokes. It is an episodic story, not in the least realistic – carefully avoiding, for instance, any of the unpleasant things you might expect to see when floods go down – but with a good deal of sly satire. When the animals get to the Zoo they find that the monkeys there are carrying on a parody of human society and organization; Stanley discovers *what* he is but realizes that the point is *who* he is; and the friends return to QV 66 to carry on exploring. To travel hopefully, it's clear, is a better thing than to arrive. There is a good deal of what might be called reversible humour: the animals' comments on what people did and how they used things make one think the animals are funny – until one changes sides, looks at people from a non-people viewpoint, and perceives that people themselves are funny, or on occasion unfunny, for instance in devising 'sharp sticks for killing each other with'. *The Voyage of QV 66* seems as I write (before publication) to have the qualities required for great popularity; and it looks a natural for an animated film.

I feel sure, however, that Penelope Lively will return, and very likely keep on returning, to the group of themes that have underlain the main body of her work. She is not likely to exhaust them. Continuity of course does not stop short at the present moment; it runs from the past through the present and on into the future. Mrs Lively has not so far engaged in any serious speculation on the future, and perhaps would have to be a different kind of writer in order to do so. She takes the matter no farther than the remaining lifespan of people now alive, but she does occasionally show children becoming aware of their own future, contemplating the (to them surprising) possibility of changing, becoming adult, growing old. Maria in *A Stitch in Time* ponders the prospect of growing into someone different, and into her head comes the idea of 'mysterious and interesting future Marias, larger and older, doing things one could barely picture'. Clare in *The House in Norham Gardens* similarly tries to project herself forward in time to meet the unknown future woman with her own name and face; but 'she walked away, the woman, a stranger, familiar and yet unreachable. The only thing you could know about her for certain was that all this would be part of her: this room, this conversation, the aunts.'

A Sounding of Storytellers

The longest and most splendid projection into the future however is Clare's birthday present to Aunt Susan. It is a copper beech tree that will take fifty years to grow and will last another two or three hundred years after that. What could more suitable for an old lady of eighty-one? There's continuity for you. Aunt Susan is delighted.

Penelope Lively

Penelope Lively writes:

I came late to writing – late and, it now seems to me, by accident. I can never answer that stock and dreaded question: how did you come to write? I fell into it, by luck rather than contrivance, on the way to somewhere quite different.

Now, looking at the publication date on my first book, I see I've been at it for ten years. Ten years, thirteen books for children, three for adults; I must have worked hard, I realize with a slight jolt. And yet it has never really felt like that: there's been time for a great deal else besides. And what has come out of it? What have I learned?

I've learned how to do the job better, I think – I hope. I've learned about the jealous conservation and nurturing of an idea – not to let it anywhere near the typewriter until it has seethed around in the mind for months, years even. I write fast once I start, but that is the end of the process: it is what has been going on before that counts. I feel like a trout hatchery sometimes – a repository for vulnerable fry in various stages of underdevelopment. I've learned to plan and shape and discard and respond to that odd intuitive feeling – which I don't think one always recognizes in early writing days – that tells you, this is right, or that is wrong. I've learned to pack it in when it's going really badly – and to go and dig the garden, or read, or distract a friend, or admire the landscape – without succumbing to despair and the conviction that things will never pick up again. They always have done before: they will. If that is learning some kind of professionalism, then up to a point I've learned that.

For years I felt diffident about describing myself as a writer: I could never put the word in those 'Occupation' spaces on forms. (The diffidence may also have been crafty sense of self-preservation – I forget how long ago it was that a neighbour said, kindly, 'Tell me, I've been wondering, do you do anything or are you just a writer?') But if everything you go about, day in and day out, all the time, is contributory in some way or another to writing, then you are a writer, and that's all there is to it: no point in being coy.

A Sounding of Storytellers

So – I've learned, and I've changed in the process. My preoccupations have shifted, diversified, sent me off in unexpected directions. I write also for adults now – not simply because some of the things I want to write about wouldn't be interesting to children. And then at other times the only possible way to tell the tale is in the form of a children's book, and with relish I change key again.

I have no working methods – except to try to pack thirty hours into twenty-four, because for every stint at the typewriter I need twice as long for talking, and listening, and reading, and generally paying attention to the world. I never know where the next book is coming from; but I've learned that it probably will come, and when it does it will be unprompted, quite likely unexpected, and all I can do is be ready and waiting.

William Mayne

William Mayne was born in Yorkshire in 1928, the eldest of five children of a doctor and a nurse. He went to Canterbury Cathedral Choir School, which provided the setting for four of his books. Since leaving school, he has taught for a brief period, travelled, and worked for a year with the B.B.C., but mostly he has been a full-time writer. He now lives in a village near Wensleydale in Yorkshire. William Mayne was awarded the Carnegie Medal for A Grass Rope *(1957), and his more recent books include* The Jersey Shore *(1973),* A Year and a Day *(1976) and* It *(1977).*

As these words are written, William Mayne has been a published author for a quarter of a century. His early work for children predates that of any other British or American writer discussed in this book. Since 1953 he has written some fifty books at a rate which still averages two a year, although there has been some slowing-up in the 1970s. He started young, and it seems reasonable to suppose that he is still in mid-career. His writing life spans a period in which there has been great development in English children's literature; in which the number of good books has greatly increased, many new writers have shot into prominence, new standards of assessment have been put forward and argued about, fashions in approach and subject-matter have changed. Mayne himself has developed, gone through phases, and appeared from time to time to change direction. Yet he has always been there, almost a fixed star in the firmament: a writer by whose qualities of sensibility, style and imagination others can be measured.

His name has always, however, been one that is likely to start an argument among adults with an interest in children's books.

A Sounding of Storytellers

It is much the same argument as the one that arises from mention of Enid Blyton, though approached from the opposite end. Enid Blyton's books are popular with great numbers of children but deeply disliked by interested adults. William Mayne appeals strongly to adults but frequently fails to arouse a response in children, even highly intelligent ones. 'A marvellous children's writer for grown-ups,' I heard it said of him years ago, 'but is he such a marvellous children's writer for children?' And impressionistic but pretty consistent evidence leads me still to believe that his books are enjoyed by a higher proportion of teachers and librarians than of children themselves.

To say this is not necessarily to make an adverse criticism. Most works of literary or other art are a minority taste, but we do not condemn them on that account. And we have no means of weighing a superficial pleasure given to many thousands against a deep personal experience which may come only to a few. My own conviction is that if a book opens windows in the imagination of only one child, it has justified its existence. Nevertheless, a limitation of appeal can be an indication that some vital element is missing. In many of Mayne's books, especially those published before the present decade, there is a lack of robustness and red corpuscle, and a tendency to shy away from the passions. Children feel strong emotion and can be deeply conscious of strong emotion in others, even when it is not understood. Life without it is less than the whole of life. 'Pity and terror,' I noted in 1971, 'are rare in Mayne's books; the expression of love, in any of its many forms, is to the best of my recollection absent.'

This observation would now be harder to sustain. It has been notable that in three or four books of the 1970s Mayne has plunged into deeper waters emotionally. His novels for older children can now be seen to to fall into four or five rough groups. There are the early treasure-hunts, beginning with his first book and reaching what must surely be the limit in ingenuity and complexity with *The Twelve Dancers* in 1962. There are the four choir school stories, which also belong to the 1950s and early 1960s. (The best of these, *A Swarm in May*

William Mayne

(1955), has treasure-hunt elements, too.) In the mid-1960s came *Sand* (1964) and *Pig in the Middle* (1965), which were about the everyday lives of boys and young adolescents, doing quite ordinary things with no elaborate mysteries to be solved. With *Earthfasts* in 1966, Mayne at last made use of the supernatural, which previously he seemed to have avoided; the fantasy element continued with *Over the Hills and Far Away* in 1968, and has remained a strand in subsequent books, often in the form of dream or vision. And lastly, beginning with *Ravensgill* in 1970, have come the books of Mayne's maturity, the deeper explorations of human nature and relationships.

Alongside the more notable books have always gone a number of lesser works. This is to be expected in a prolific writer. In a short essay like the present one, it is impossible to discuss them all. I shall confine my comments to a few major or landmark books; others may be mentioned in passing or not at all.

A writer's first book is a landmark by virtue of being first, even if in comparison with later work it does not seem particularly important. *Follow the Footprints*, which appeared in 1953 when Mayne was only twenty-five, is characteristic in many ways and could hardly be mistaken for the work of anyone else. It is the first of those elaborate treasure-hunts: a story in which reputedly supernatural phenomena – the warm footprints of a saint – turn out to have a rational explanation, and in which a mystery from the past is triumphantly solved. It is not yet vintage Mayne; he was to do the same thing in several later books, and do it better. And, uncharacteristically, it has a villain: a rogue with the suitably unpleasant-sounding name of Squenn. But it is full of typical Mayne dialogue:

'I can see the sea,' said Caroline. 'Quite easily.'
Everybody came to look. To the south, at the farthest edge of sight there was the thin blue shading that showed the sea, and beyond that the sky.
'Funny how you can always see something,' said Andrew. 'Even if it's not really there, like the sky.'
'The sky's there,' said Caroline.

141

'It isn't,' said Andrew. 'You can see it, but there's nothing there.'

'That's the sea all right,' said Daddy. 'And after that there's Ireland, then America.'

'Then Australia,' said Andrew. 'Then Siberia, then we get back here again. So we're really looking at the back of our own heads.'

This passage from the fourth page of Mayne's first book is no doubt an early instance of what a reviewer in *The Times Literary Supplement* twenty years later was to call 'the whimsical chit-chat that is the most dispensable part of his writing'. But for better or worse it has the authentic Mayne flavour.

I did not read *Follow the Footprints* when it first came out, so I cannot say how it seemed when Mayne was new and when the number of good current children's books was much smaller. I do however recall the first appearance in 1955 of *A Swarm in May*, which seemed then, and seems now, an outstanding piece of work. In this novel, set in a cathedral choir school based on the one he had attended as a boy, Mayne created or re-created a closed, complete and satisfying world, in which a large cast of characters were clearly distinguished, and in which a story was intriguingly told and a mystery satisfyingly solved. And behind these individuals, behind the daily life of school and the puzzle from the past, emerging out of the mist to dwarf them all, was the cathedral itself. Indeed, the cathedral seemed in the end to become the frame of the story: a frame filled with cathedral space, a space filled with cathedral music, with the choir's singing and Dr Sunderland's organ-playing.

Considered as a young man's book, *A Swarm in May* can hardly be faulted. But after it came a period in which Mayne seemed to be elegantly treading water. Individually his books were of obvious distinction and were duly acclaimed, but collectively they began to add up to a disappointment. Three more choir school stories – *Choristers' Cake* (1956), *Cathedral Wednesday* (1960), and *Words and Music* (1963) – followed *A Swarm in May*. There were more treasure-hunts, too. *A Grass Rope* (1957), to which I shall return later, was the best of these, and won the Carnegie Medal. With *The Thumbstick* (1959), *The Rolling Season* (1960) and *The Twelve Dancers* the treasure-hunts grew ever more convoluted, and the author himself presumably realized that he had reached the end of that particular road.

By the middle of the 1960s, there was a movement in British children's books towards stories about the everyday contemporary life of ordinary families. This may well be reflected in *Sand* and *Pig in the Middle*. *Sand* especially might form a good introduction to Mayne's work for the child who, while not a reluctant reader, might be put off by some of the more mannered or more demanding of his books. Here – a new departure for Mayne – we have a group of boys who are desperately keen to get to know some girls, though they don't quite know how to set about it. Excavating the tracks of an old narrow-gauge railway might not seem the most promising approach, but it leads to a pleasing and humorous climax in which the boys – an idiosyncratic bunch – dump a huge, supposedly-prehistoric skeleton in the girls' school yard by way of getting acquainted. The setting of *Sand* is a Yorkshire coast town that is being slowly suffocated by sand-dunes; the sand can almost be felt on the reader's eyeballs; and there is a memorable relationship between the hero Ainsley and the elder sister who refers to him disdainfully in his presence: 'Look at him laying the jam on,' said Alice. 'Doesn't it disgust you, Mother?' I have heard praise of *Pig in the Middle*, a story about boys in an inner-city district who try to rehabilitate an old barge; but although this operation is convincingly described it seems to me that Mayne is not at home in his setting.

Then in 1966 came a major new departure with *Earthfasts*, an exceptionally fine book in which William Mayne at last surpassed his early work. Here he not only used the supernatural but used it to splendid effect. There are no excursions into 'secondary worlds', as in Tolkien or C. S. Lewis; *Earthfasts*, in the manner of Alan Garner, brings the fantasy element into a solid contemporary setting; and to make it more credible Mayne has as his main characters two modern, scientifically-minded schoolboys who look for rational explanations of everything. When *they* are convinced that the impossible has happened, we are all convinced.

A Sounding of Storytellers

On a Yorkshire hillside one evening, David and Keith see a stirring in the turf and hear a drumming; there's movement as if someone was getting out of bed, there's light, 'increasing light, pure and mild and bleak', and out of the hillside marches a drummer-boy who'd marched into it in 1742 and hadn't been heard of since. He carries a candle that burns with a cold, white, unchanging flame, and he has been searching for the supposed burial-place of King Arthur and his knights. The drummer is a matter-of-fact Yorkshire lad, and he marches off to look for the cottage where he used to live – which is still there – and the girl he left behind him – who is not. When the boys convince him of his situation he doesn't make too much fuss but marches back into the hillside.

The drummer-boy's appearance resulted from something like a geological fault in time. Over the next few weeks there are strange phenomena: huge footprints appear, a wild boar roams the streets, prehistoric stones move from their places – but are they stones or giants? Strangest yet, David, by looking into that cold candlelight, acquires some kind of second sight, more a danger than a gift; and one day he vanishes from the earth – struck, people think, by lightning. From here the story, like some swift, intricate dance, swirls eye-defeatingly faster and faster until the moment when Keith, replacing the cold-flamed candle in the centre of a round table in an underground cavern, stops everything, turns moving figures into stalactite and stalagmite, and seals up the fault in time.

The sheer sweep of *Earthfasts*, swift and wide and totally under control, has never been matched by Mayne. It also seems to have begun a new lease of artistic life. In 1968 he took up another time theme but played it the other way round, with his present-day characters journeying into the past. This was *Over the Hills and Far Away*, in which Dolly and Andrew and Sara, pony-trekking on a visit to their Gran, find themselves switched into post-Roman Britain, into a tale of old unhappy far-off things that they can't understand or even really believe in. And Sara, who has flaming red hair, is looked on by the tribesmen among whom she finds herself as a witch, a saviour, a

sacrifice. *Over the Hills and Far Away* is notable for an outstandingly clear, almost transparent style of writing, and for the
effective contrast between the fluid, dreamlike nature of the
action and the enduring solidity of the Yorkshire landscape
through which it moves.

Ravensgill marks a further development. It is not so spectacular a new departure as *Earthfasts*, but it is not less significant. The
setting, yet again, is that Yorkshire dalescape which is Mayne's
own country; and at first sight *Ravensgill* bears some resemb-
lance to the books of the *Grass Rope* period, a dozen years
earlier. Geographically, the places named in *Ravensgill* and those
in *A Grass Rope* are close together: Vendale (a name given by
Charles Kingsley to the dale in which the runaway chimney-
sweep Tom arrives in *The Water Babies*) forms part of the
background of both. There is a superficial similarity of plot
between *Ravensgill* and *A Grass Rope*; in each of them a problem
from the past is solved by young people of the present day, and
in each case a newly-formed boy-girl friendship is involved in
the solution. But to put the two books side by side is to see the
difference.

The mystery from which the action of *A Grass Rope* arises is
buried a long way back in the past. It is a romantic story, of a
girl's being carried off against her father's will, from which any
emotional resonances have long since faded away. The traces
that survive into the present are harmless: families who still bear
the names of ancient opponents now live in casual and unself-
conscious amity; names given to dogs, and the name and sign of
an old inn, contain clues to the solution of a puzzle; and a puzzle
to be solved is all that it is. *A Grass Rope* is a happy book about
people whom it is a pleasure to meet, in a landscape one is glad
to visit; and its denouement, approached at a leisurely pace, is
satisfying when reached. To read *Ravensgill* is not a more
enjoyable experience than to read *A Grass Rope*, but it is a deeper
and richer one.

There is a sombre note in *Ravensgill* which is new to Mayne.
Here the mystery is an unsolved crime of half a century ago, still
casting its malign influence on the related families at two farms,

not many miles apart yet totally estranged. Discovery by two young people, Bob and Judith, of an underground way from Vendale to Ravensgill now proves that Lizzie White's husband was innocent of the crime with which he was charged all those years ago, when Lizzie herself was young. But it is too late; the damage is done; the impetuous girl who lost her man has changed with the passage of time into Grandma, a foolish, pathetic, though still spirited, old woman.

One senses in *Ravensgill* that the air is full of old guilt and fear, grievance and pain and loss. There is a marvellous chapter in which Bob cycles to York to seek out the widow of the policeman who had kept the murder case open for many years, and spends a day of blazing heat in an atmosphere in which all touch with reality has been lost; he is as far from his own daily life as he is from the long-forgotten crime. Yet it is arguable that even in *Ravensgill* Mayne is still holding back; he is aware of deep feeling, but he defines it by drawing round its edges. One is never quite there in the middle, experiencing the full emotional charge.

In *A Game of Dark* (1971) a boy's inability to cope with an emotional overload is actually the matter of the book. Donald, nearly fifteen, has troubles enough to overwhelm anyone: a sternly Methodist, dying father whom he cannot love; a mother of similar outlook who teaches at his school and who addresses him there, and sometimes at home too, by his surname; a friendship, bitterly resented by his parents, with the Anglican vicar, whose chumminess has homosexual overtones and who was indirectly responsible for his sister's death and his father's maiming in an accident. With his father drawing nearer to death, his own inability to love or even communicate growing ever more shocking to himself, and his friend the Rev. 'Berry' Braxham on the point of leaving for another parish, Donald switches off from reality with increasing frequency, and moves into a fantasy world in which he is a squire, serving a lord whose duty it is to kill the huge, stinking, marauding Worm that preys on a medieval town. When the lord himself is killed, it falls to Donald to deal with the Worm; and this he does, not in fair

combat but by stabbing its under-belly from a hole in the
ground. It is 'not an honourable deed'; but now he can return to
and accept the real world and can love his father, who dies
almost at once. 'There was no more breathing. Donald lay and
listened to the quiet, and went to sleep, consolate.'

Clearly Donald's fantasy results from extreme emotional
disturbance, but it serves its purpose; the end of the story,
though harrowing, shows him restored to mental health. To
examine in detail the psychology and symbolism of the fantasy
world would be impossible here, and probably unfruitful anyway. The lord whom Donald serves as squire is explicitly
identified with the clergyman. The Worm has Biblical and
mythological associations; in its context one takes it to be a
compound of Donald's monstrous guilt, of his father's enormous ugly pain, and also – in Freudian terms – of Father himself.

There is strong stuff here, and the novel had an understandably mixed reception. I feel myself that it is uneasily situated on
the children's list. Like Alan Garner's *Red Shift*, it makes high
demands on a young reader. In this case the requirement is for
more emotional and literary experience, more acquaintance
with psychological theory, than can reasonably be expected of
children and young adolescents. And while one hesitates to
suggest that readers should be sheltered from harsh reality – the
trend of children's literature in recent years has been steadily
away from this view – it may be better that some kinds of
literary experience should come as part of young people's reaching out into the adult world, the reading they do at their own
risk, so to speak, rather than in books which are classified as
children's reading and appear on the shelves of the children's
library. *A Game of Dark* has nightmare in it: the kind of nightmare that can lurk for a long time in the corners of the mind.

The book of depth and feeling that really works, and surely
Mayne's best up to this point, is *The Jersey Shore* (1973). In
outline it is very simple. Arthur, an American boy staying on
the coast of New Jersey in the 1930s, meets his grandfather,
who came from England and was married three times, though
never to the girl he really loved. Grandfather talks to Arthur as

he does to no one else. He tells of old unhappy far-off things, of rural poverty and hardship, of wives and children who died, in a land of sea and fen and the fever called marsh-drench; and he also hands on knowledge expressed in shared dream or vision rather than words. In an epilogue Arthur, now grown-up Art, flies to England with the United States Air Force, visits Grandfather's country, and completes the link that Grandfather could not. This is a book in which the English landscape and the old rural way of life, the sense of patient suffering, the mysteries of time and kinship and memory are woven marvellously together.

Besides his novels, William Mayne has written a number of shorter books for young children. His stories of everyday life for the younger age group are indeed among the best in that rather barren genre. A pleasure in fantasy can be shared by writer, parent and quite small child; but most authors seem to find it difficult to tell a worthwhile story for younger children about actual life. *No More School* (1965), which tells how Ruth and Shirley keep the village school unofficially open while the teacher Miss Oldroyd is ill, is a small gem of a story, for all that there is nothing in it beyond the understanding of a child of eight or nine. *The Toffee Join* (1968) is about three sets of cousins and the contributions they take to the sweet-making of their joint Granny; it is perfectly on the level of a small child, and it is perfectly and properly serious. There are several others. Mayne's special quality as a writer for young children is that he never sees things with the used adult eye, or fails to see them because of the preoccupied adult mind. Everything is experienced afresh. He notes exactly the things that children do but adults have forgotten: '"It's raining," said Diana. She huffed her breath on to the window and drew on the steamy mark with her finger. She drew a smile and a nose and two eyes, but before she could draw the chin and the hair and the ears the mark had gone away.' That is the opening of *The Toffee Join*. A few pages on, Mother is giving the children treacle in a polythene bag. It sits 'all smiling in the clear plastic', and each child in turn has to have the cold clingy bag pressed against the back of its neck.

William Mayne

There is never any condescension, and nothing about the small details of daily life is dull or commonplace.

Whether *A Year and a Day* (1976) counts as a book for young children I am not sure. I am not sure whether it counts as fantasy either; the better the book, the less such classifications matter. This is the brief beautiful story of the tiny naked boy with dark hair and dark eyes and skin like milk whom Sara and Becca, small cottage children in Cornwall a century or more ago, find 'sitting in a grassy tangle like a nest'. He doesn't speak, but he can imitate any sound he hears. The local wise woman, Janey Tregose, says he is a fairy child, here for a year and a day only; and so it proves. They call him Adam; he thrives at first, but pines as the year draws on, and when the time is up the children find him 'sleeping cold'. This is a story of loving care: the two little girls love Adam; the parents, poor cottage folk, love all of them. The telling is limpid and tender. The children are not unhappy at the end; they are sure that in some way he is with them still, and soon Mother has a second Adam, a fine lusty boy, as consolation. If, as may be the case, there once were inhibitions which kept the human warmth in Mayne from being fully expressed on the page, *A Year and a Day* makes it clear that the barriers now are down.

This last opening-up may have been what he most needed to add to an impressive array of talents. He has a genuinely original if sometimes unduly whimsical mind. He writes superbly. He has a fine imagination, and a gift for story construction and narration when he cares to use it. He knows how things are done, and can tell you. He can evoke a landscape, a time of day or year, a kind of weather, the feeling of the way things are, as in *Sand*: 'The shirt was made of cold cloth and frozen buttons. It lay on Ainsley's bed like a drift of snow. The cold spring wind blew the curtains and moaned under the door. Ainsley stroked the shirt. It had been starched with ice.' He has an unfailing gift for the precise and vivid simile: 'Her heart banged in her like a wildcat in a sack', or 'The flame perched on the wick like a bright bird' (both from *Over the Hills and Far Away*). He is a notable writer of dialogue, and, like many who excel in this field, appears to have a gift of mimicry. His books pick up the ways of speech of the places in which they are set: in *The Twelve Dancers*, for instance, almost all the characters are Welsh, and although not a word of Welsh is spoken, their English is Welsh English. His ear is impeccable, and one hardly needs to be told that he is a musical man. The unfailing ear and the aptitude for dialogue and mimicry have combined in recent books with remarkable effect: the voices of the old man in *The Jersey Shore*, or of the maid-servant Kate who tells the story of *Max's Dream* (1977), are unique and individual, and of course help to establish their characters; to a great extent they *are* the words they use.

A rereading of many of Mayne's books leaves me feeling that when all is said and done he is probably still the most gifted of contemporary British children's writers. His early promise was fulfilled long ago. But perhaps it is a sign of a major and lasting talent that it continues to raise expectations; that there is never a point at which one thinks, 'He might as well sit back now; he had made his contribution.' Mayne has gone on promising: promising afresh, so to speak, as new facets of his talent were revealed; and he is abundantly promising still.

William Mayne

William Mayne writes:

My ways of doing things are either so boring that they don't bear retailing, or so private that even I do not know about them. I don't see why anyone shouldn't do it, because it's reasonably easy, but if I say so then anyone thinks I am being arrogant. The boring bits are the getting up every twenty-four hours or so and walking to the typewriter, or pen, or dictating machine, or telephone if the controls of other devices are too complex that day, and uttering a few words. All I can consciously do is be present, somewhat but not toowhat awake, clothed and (by various tests taken daily) sane enough to mix with humanity. It is possible to be too insane, relatively speaking; that is, sane by some median internal judgement, not having become proud, or certain, or angry, not hating or envying or assessing. I am only a lens for others, and I must do my best not to distort or colour. My responsibility for being the *lens sana* goes only so far, though, as far as seeing that what I say is what I see. I am not responsible for what I see, though I can be blamed for what I look at. And since I am not responsible there I am not responsible either for what anyone else sees. If the lens is astigmatic I may not know it; chromatic aberrations too are not detectable from within the organism, where I am *in corpore sano*, perhaps, perhaps not.

I have no ambitions in writing. I may have a few plots in mind at any moment, but that's not ambition. My daily care is not for *what* I may do, but *how* I may do it. My future writing is not of interest to me, because interest in it now might be a substitute for experiencing it then, when the time comes to write it. I am quite out of the habit of telling anyone what I am doing, have done, or hope to do. A thing once said ought not to be said again, if possible, and to say now would preclude later writing; to think now might do the same. An attitude of mind like that is probably a hindrance to writing, and a positive impediment to plotting. I must use some other method. I am not clear what it is, however. I can only abstract the observed cycle, that I think of something, then I write it down, then I don't think of anything for some time, and then I think of something else, and so on. Actually of course I am thinking of several things at once, but usually only writing down one at a time. I don't like writing. I decided on it as a career when I was too young to realize I would not grow out of the dislike, but I have never had enough imagination to think of another living. But I suppose the same rules would apply whatever I did: the rules we all are aware of.

Jill Paton Walsh

Jill Paton Walsh was born in London in 1937 and was educated there and at St Anne's College, Oxford. She taught for a while before beginning to write, and is now the author of a novel for adults as well as several books for young readers. Her first book, Hengest's Tale, *was published in 1966, and those that have followed include* Fireweed *(1969),* Goldengrove *(1972),* Unleaving *(1976) and A* Chance Child *(1978). She received a Whitbread Literary Award for* The Emperor's Winding Sheet *in 1974. Jill Paton Walsh lives with her husband and three children in Richmond, Surrey.*

Jill Paton Walsh is a writer with powerful driving force and at the same time with fine and subtle perceptions. She has the historical imagination to a rare degree and carries a great deal of learning lightly. She is a descriptive writer with a precise visual sense and an admirable ear. And she can catch the fleeting moment: what she calls in *Unleaving* (1976) 'the eternal aspect of the momentary now'. In the distribution of the talents she has been dealt, so to speak, a formidable hand. It is not surprising that she is versatile and has written several kinds of book, including some that cut across the boundaries of the conventional genres.

She sees narrative as a vital element in fiction, and has pointed out that children's writers who seek to tell a good story are 'working in a literary tradition that goes back not to *Ulysses* but to Odysseus'.[1] The gift which was least evident in her early work was the novelist's ability to create character through dialogue; but to read her books in order of publication is to see

1. Jill Paton Walsh, 'The Rainbow Surface', *The Times Literary Supplement*, 3 December, 1971, reprinted in *The Cool Web*, ed. Meek and others (Bodley Head, 1977; Atheneum, 1978), pp. 192–5.

153

that she has developed this ability greatly with experience. She has become more of a novelist as her career has gone on, without ever ceasing to be a storyteller.

She does not shun the big scene of action; it could be said of her, as has been said of Rosemary Sutcliff, that she 'will always put down her harp for a battle'.[2] War, and the pity of war, has often been her subject; but besides the waste and agony of it, she also has a sense of the heroism that flowers in wartime, the terrible splendour. She has a proper respect for physical courage. Her first book, *Hengest's Tale* (1966), has indeed a kind of bloody magnificence, recalling inevitably *Beowulf* and the Sagas. The Romans have gone, and we are among the barbarians of northern Europe: Jutes, Frisians, Danes. And it is a fearful story of fighting, quarrelling, betrayal, murder; of noble concepts of loyalty to lord or kin which result in – and in fact enforce – the wreck of love and friendship, the destruction of life. Slaughter breeds slaughter, and the most dreadful moments are those when the lust for blood takes over, culminating in Hengest's slaying his friend and going berserk, not knowing how many he kills.

Men of course are the victims of their appalling ideals; Hengest is left with grim and bitter memories, the death of the heart. And yet he looks to his violent deeds for immortality: 'I will tell you what I have done, so that you may make a fine song out of it, and keep my name alive after my death.' The author has put together her story from 'the broken pieces of an old one'; there is a ruthlessness in her telling that matches her material, and she has indeed made a fine, if terrible, song out of it. I personally find *Hengest's Tale* uncongenial in the extreme, and would not read it for pleasure. But it is undeniably impressive. The author who, writing for children, could piece together this fierce and testing tale was alarmingly talented; and she was not yet thirty years old.

Jill Paton Walsh's second book was again a war story, but she had jumped from the Dark Ages to 1940. *The Dolphin Crossing*

2. Review quoted by Margaret Meek in *Rosemary Sutcliff* (Bodley Head Monograph, 1962), p. 55.

(1967) has more of the awkwardness of early work than *Hengest's Tale*. The action theme, the rescue of British troops from Dunkirk, is brilliantly handled, with the unsparing realism that the author has already displayed. But *The Dolphin Crossing* is deficient in the creation of people who live and breathe, the development of patterns of relationship between them, the effects of experience on character. In *Hengest's Tale*, as in epic and saga generally, people are simple: brave or cowardly, loyal or treacherous as the case may be. What they are is determined by what they have to do. In *The Dolphin Crossing*, where the Dunkirk rescue takes up only a third of the book and the rest is set in the context of dull civilian life in early wartime Britain, there is a need to make people and their responses to each other and to circumstances interesting; and the author is, I think, still feeling her way.

Some of the first two-thirds of *The Dolphin Crossing* in fact make uneasy reading. John Aston, from whose point of view the story is mainly told, has in him a good deal of the conventional hero of old-fashioned boys' fiction. At times he is high-minded to the point of priggishness. Telling his newly-made friend, the London evacuee Pat, of his plan to join the Dunkirk fleet with his father's boat *Dolphin*, John warns him: 'We might get killed. In fact we'll probably get killed. Nobody will be defending us. It couldn't be a more dangerous thing to do. But England isn't short of boys like us; she is short of trained soldiers.' Though the author intended John to be an admirable character, she has acknowledged that he emerges as 'a pompous stiff-shirted boy who leads a tender-hearted, vulnerable, rather stupid one into a dangerous corner'. It is in fact Pat who is more likeable and more interesting. For most of its course, *The Dolphin Crossing* is a mediocre book. But it is redeemed when the action takes over. Then one ceases to observe John and identifies with him instead. Class differences between him and Pat cease to be embarrassing; the boys are two in the same boat, representatives of all of us, struggling to survive and win through.

Fireweed (1969) shows an astonishing advance upon *The*

Dolphin Crossing. Again it is a war novel: the story of a boy and girl on the run in the London blitz. One would not have doubted this author's ability to deal with the blitz, but here she goes far beyond expectations. The blitz is a background, albeit an important and spectacular one, to the personal story of Bill and Julie; and Jill Paton Walsh achieves something more remarkable than realism: that sense of unreality-in-reality when the things that are actually happening are beyond everyday belief. So although the noise, the fitful vivid illumination of blazing London, the sheer physical impact are all present, and indeed are battering vicariously at the senses, the reader can also move with Bill and Julie in a world of their own, almost dreamlike, where the gentler, intensely personal emotions of loving and caring take refuge and survive.

In the brief flowering of their relationship, this boy and girl make a home in the cellar of a bombed building and act out a semblance of adult life: earning money, looking after a lost child. This is a story not of adolescent sexuality but of love: a love that might be thought premature in a couple of fifteen-year-olds if it were not brought forward by the precarious circumstances of their survival, their responsibility for each other. It is innocent love, but it achieves a symbolic consummation, in a passage which is both delicate and lyrical, when the girl, cold at night, comes to sleep in the boy's arms. Next morning they are happy, and it seems to Bill, who is the narrator, that 'we hadn't come apart properly when we rose from sleep, but in some way we moved together still'.

It cannot last. Julie, buried when the cellar collapses, is rescued and returned to her parents, and after one brief hospital visit Bill will never see her again. At this point there is possibly a slight failure of credibility; one does not quite believe that the class barriers would close around Julie so swiftly and decisively, or that these devoted youngsters would have allowed themselves to be separated without a struggle. But if this is a flaw it is a superficial one; the shape of the story is right, the parting has to take place, for ephemerality is of the essence of this relationship.

Jill Paton Walsh

Jill Paton Walsh has herself defined an historical novel as one that is 'wholly or partly about the public events and social conditions which are the material of history, regardless of the time at which it is written'.[3] She has said that her two Second World War books are not true historical novels because 'they are really about courage and first love in times of crisis; I could easily have set them in other wars, other places, without changing the emotional core'. In the early 1970s, however, she wrote two novels which are indisputably and thoroughly historical: *Farewell Great King*[4] (1972) and *The Emperor's Winding Sheet* (1974). The former was published as an adult novel, the latter on the children's list; and *The Emperor* is clearly designed to be a children's book in that the author has placed a boy in the centre of her story and has narrated it largely from his eye level. There is however no obvious reason inherent in the subject-matter itself for making one of the two a children's book and not the other.

Farewell Great King is an account of Greek, especially Athenian, history at and around the time of the Persian Wars (fifth century B.C.). It takes the form of an apologia addressed at the end of his life by Themistocles, the Athenian general and victor of Salamis, to the Persian King Artaxerxes, with whom Themistocles had taken service. It adheres closely to the known facts, and the people in it are actual people. Being shaped by the events it describes and by the autobiographical form, it is as constrained as a work of fiction well could be. A great deal of its interest indeed lies in the history rather than the fiction: in the recurrent, astonished realization that these things did actually happen, that these Greeks really did defeat the Persian hordes, that so many patterns of our own lives, so many of our political problems and preoccupations, can be seen prefigured in fifth-century Athens. Themistocles, the wily democrat and demagogue, who lined his own pockets but saved Athens, who

3. Jill Paton Walsh, 'History is Fiction', *Horn Book*, February 1972, reprinted in *Crosscurrents of Criticism*, ed. Heins (The Horn Book Inc., 1977) pp. 219–25.

4. *Farewell Great King* (London, Macmillan, 1972).

was banished by his fellow-citizens and went over to the arch-enemy, is one of history's intriguingly ambiguous figures. As hero he would not be everybody's choice; would not be mine.

The Emperor's Winding Sheet, about the siege of Constantinople and its final fall to the Turks, is a novel of high excellence: quite possibly the best historical novel to be published on any British list, adult or children's, in its decade. Again it gives a faithful account of historical events, but it is a more satisfying novel than *Farewell Great King*: partly because the pattern of those events is one of drama, indeed of high tragedy. The emperor of this book is the last Constantine; his winding sheet is the city itself, the remnant of empire; he is identified with it, and his personal tragedy is also that of the city and indeed of a civilization.

It is a demanding novel, by no means an easy read. The visualization of Constantinople – precise, detailed, and continuing all through the narrative – is rewarding to careful attention and crucial to a full appreciation of the book, but to a slipshod reader it could be merely wordage. The theological arguments, diplomatic manoeuvrings and battles on land and sea require to be followed carefully; a large cast needs to be remembered; and from all this maze of activity and description emerges the detailed portrait of the Emperor himself, the dominant figure. The Emperor must be equal to his role in the tragedy; and he is. He is in fact a study in nobility, which is as hard a quality to portray convincingly as anything in fiction.

Vrethiki, the lucky find – otherwise Piers Barber, the boy from Bristol – is conscripted as the Emperor's personal attendant in response to a prophecy. This is a skilful piece of fictional management: not only does Vrethiki provide a boy's-eye-view of the story, but he has good reason to be present when things are happening, and he has to have matters explained to him. The limitations of his understanding are turned into strengths. Whether the introduction of an English boy is enough to make the story attractive to the run of reading children is another question. Vrethiki is not in fact a perfect instrument. He cannot be allowed to play a significant part in the action; he can only observe. And he is necessarily pushed aside from time to time when the matter to be conveyed is such that a boy – and a foreign boy at that – could not have understood it. At other times he has feelings attributed to him which are not consistent with his age and experience, as when he attends a service of union in the great Church of Santa Sophia.

'What does it matter?' thought Vrethiki. 'What does any of it matter, compared to this? Churches at home are like hands, human hands laid together in prayer and pointing upwards, but this church is like a swelling joy, like the ecstasy of the heart. Compared to this what does a *Filioque* matter, or a morsel of leaven in bread? Compared to this what do life and death matter, even mine? All that is as nothing, in the eternal wisdom of God.'

This is splendid, but it is not boyish. In the course of the book, however, Vrethiki – and perhaps by extension the reader – gets an education in the moral and practical complexity of things. And the novel as a whole shows continuing and impressive development of the author's stylistic mastery. She can make words sing. And she can use a long sentence to extraordinary effect. The second sentence of the book, for instance, moves from a single item in the foreground to indicate a whole landscape and lead back through it to the events which have preceded the opening of the story:

The orange tree stood in the garden of a great church, built at the foot of the steep little town, a town all of pink brick and rosy red stone, with narrow winding streets, steps all the way, that clung to the top of a precipitous conical hill, a foothill of the mountains through which the boy had come, in pain from hunger, in pain from cold, and driven by the terror behind him.

A similar technique is used in the magnificent closing sentence of the whole book, when Vrethiki, with the Emperor dead and nothing to be saved but himself, swims out to a Genoese vessel which will carry him towards home:

159

A Sounding of Storytellers

With her delicately-rigged moonshadow slipping along beside her, she sloped in the wind, and slid through the quiet Marmara, making for Western landfalls – for unconquered islands, and safe Christian anchorages, and so to far-distant Genoa, whence the Atlantic merchantmen embark their goods and men for England, in her cold northern seas.

The ability to combine the visual, the sounding and the evocative is most evident of all in Jill Paton Walsh's pair of novels set on the Cornish coast some time around the present day: *Goldengrove* (1972) and *Unleaving*. The titles, of course, form a quotation from a poem on 'Spring and Fall: To a Young Child' by Gerard Manley Hopkins:

> Margaret, are you grieving
> Over Goldengrove unleaving? . . .
> Ah, as the heart grows, older
> It will come to such sights colder
> By and by, nor spare a sigh
> Though worlds of wanwood leafmeal lie . . .
> It is the blight man was born for.
> It is Margaret you mourn for.

And the poem does provide a key – if key is needed – to the first book, *Goldengrove*, which is largely about the cost of growing up, the loss of childhood. Madge, whose full name is Margaret, has stayed year after year with Paul, supposedly her cousin, at Gran's house at St Ives. This year all is changing. She and Paul cannot share a room any more; their relationship is not what it was when both were children (and yet he is still so young, totally a boy). And there is the blind professor staying near by, to whom she can read; to whose Rochester perhaps she can be Jane. But nothing works out. Paul, it transpires, is her brother, the brother whom once she needed badly but of whom she was deprived by parental strife; now it is too late, and she only feels that she has lost him afresh. And Professor Ashton, whose wife left him after he was blinded in the war, has retreated behind locked doors of self, rejecting love and kindness, refusing to trust even Madge for fear of being let down, wanting nothing

160

from her but her reading voice. In his words, which she repeats at the end of the book, 'some wounds cannot be healed; some things are beyond helping and cannot be put right'.

It sounds, and in some ways it is, a sad book; but it is not as sad as may appear. The loss of childhood is after all a universal fact of life which we must all survive; and we see Madge, after some turmoil, surviving it, while for direct, spontaneous Paul there can be no fears. And although the title and the main theme come from Hopkins, the true literary correspondences are with Virginia Woolf. A fixed mark in Jill Paton Walsh's seascape is Godrevy lighthouse, the same one as in *To the Lighthouse* – of which book, we may recall, Virginia Woolf said that 'the sea is to be heard all through it'.[5] *Goldengrove* is a book full of light, of endlessly-changing sea and sky; and, as with Virginia Woolf, there is an acute – one might say exquisite – perception of the living moment which can only be joyful.

Nevertheless, *Goldengrove* is outshone by *Unleaving*, a profoundly beautiful book. The title itself is ambiguous, referring as in the Hopkins poem to the fall of leaves in autumn, but suggesting at the same time an almost opposite meaning, for 'unleaving' implies 'remaining'. In the early stages of a first reading, the book may seem difficult; there are two alternating strands of narration, and the relationship between them is not obvious. Before the end all is clear, but a second reading is desirable anyway, since the book ends in a surprise which casts fresh light on all that has gone before.

The main strand shows Madge a little older and once more at Goldengrove; for Gran has died, Madge has inherited the house and is there at the same time as an Oxford reading party to whom she has rented it. Professor Tregeagle's son Patrick, like Madge, is a creature of feeling; he cannot bear the derision faced by his small mongol sister Molly, or the suffering he foresees for her when she gets older. And while his father and the philosophy students discuss ends and means in abstract terms, Patrick drives himself towards a fearful decision. Does he, in the

5. Virginia Woolf, *A Writer's Diary* (Hogarth Press, 1954; Harcourt Brace 1973), p. 80.

event, push Molly from the edge of a cliff? Certainly he wishes to do so; she falls; and her death is followed by that of a lifeboatman in the boiling sea below. There is no restricting the consequences of our actions to the intended end alone; we are not God. Patrick goes through an intensity of suffering; Madge loves and saves him.

Parallel with this story of storm and stress, ingeniously interleaved with it, is a serene account of a calm Cornish summer in which an old lady talks to her children, watches her grandchildren play, enjoys her garden and her view, and remembers what has gone. And when the two streams of narrative flow together at the end, we see what we immediately feel we should have seen from the start. The working together of the two themes is achieved with great formal beauty; and even more than *Goldengrove* the story is full of sea, superb in all its moods; of light and landscape; the celebration of the passing but immortal moment.

It would not be easy for Jill Paton Walsh, or anyone else, to write a better book than *Unleaving*, but in *A Chance Child* (1978) she produced a novel which was remarkably different and opened up new imaginative vistas. For the first time in her work, there is a fantasy element. But there are also elements of historical fiction and of contemporary realism; the book offers in itself a quiet comment on the irrelevance of classification by genre.

The chance child, born to a woman whose husband is away, is unwanted, ill-treated, shut in a cupboard under the stairs of a house in a poor district; he doesn't even have a name, being referred to as 'that creep'. When a hole is knocked in the wall of the house, Creep escapes and wanders off along the canal bank. It is soon evident that something strange is happening; and gradually it becomes clear (the measured revelation is a fine piece of craftsmanship, making the book neither too obscure nor too obvious) that Creep has moved into the past, into the time the canal itself arises from. He encounters children, in a sense his kindred, who labour in the growing, callously-vigorous industries of early nineteenth-century England: especially Tom from the pit and Blackie who works for a nail-maker and has a lopsided face from the burns she got when she fell in the fire. Creep helps children quietly with their work, but he never eats, never laughs, and only those whose lives are hard and troubled can even see him; he is a kind of ghost from the future. The day comes when, in a cotton mill, a beaten child's mother beats the master with a billy-roller, and Creep laughs out loud. And then everyone can see him, and he is suddenly hungry; he has crossed over physically into the past. His half-brother Christopher, searching for him in chapters which alternate with the story of Creep, realizes in the end that Creep will never come back; he is safe in the past for ever.

Much of this story will make shocking reading for young people today, though they are only five or six generations removed from the children whose labours helped to feed the Industrial Revolution. But though much of it is grim, the book is never cynical or hopeless; Creep's helping hand surely symbolizes the help given by the oppressed to each other. And the author is honest: she refrains from easy indignation, aware that the advance of industry was ultimately a huge step forward for which a price had to be paid; aware, too, that those who exploited children were often working folk, sometimes their own parents. *A Chance Child* is both clear-eyed and compassionate. And Jill Paton Walsh's descriptive powers have never been put to more impressive use than here. There is a marvellous passage which tells how Creep and Blackie watch from the canal, before dawn, as the windows of a mill light up and the workers begin to arrive:

Along the canal bank people were moving. They were coming slowly, and silently, in great numbers, crossing a bridge, going all towards a lamp, just now lit, that showed to Creep and Blackie a gate into the vast windowed place. The crowd seemed to be sleep-walking, so silent were they, and so dreamlike and sluggish their pace. And some of them were little children. Little children trailing along behind larger ones, led by the hand by young women in shawls and clogs, or carried bodily in the arms of men. They came like moths out of the dark, and crossed through the pool of light at the mill door; and Creep saw one child, arms across the shoulders of two others, making walking movements with his feet, though his feet did not touch the ground, for he was supported by his friends.

It has sometimes seemed, in the years since *Fireweed*, that Jill Paton Walsh might be moving away from the children's list. Certainly *The Emperor's Winding Sheet* and *Unleaving* – to say nothing of *Farewell Great King*, and the admirable quartet of short stories 'Four Tides', included in *Young Winter's Tales* 7 [6] – require a degree of maturity unlikely to be found in those below their teens. *A Chance Child* strikes one, however, as plainly a children's book, and Jill Paton Walsh has also written several books for younger children. These include three small pendants to *Farewell Great King*, in the form of brief stories in which episodes from Themistocles' life are picked out, and fictional children are allowed to play parts in otherwise-historical events. And *The Butty Boy* (1975) tells the story of a small girl of late Victorian days who runs away to join a pair of children working a narrow-boat on the canals.

Speaking at the Exeter Conference in 1973, Jill Paton Walsh remarked that nearly all the children's books which received the highest praise were in one genre: fantasy. Yet fantasy, she suggested, was only one of the tools available to a writer, and 'it is not, and never could be, my tool'. She expressed some dissatisfaction with the kind of writing that 'floats free from reality'. The renunciation seemed surprising, as does any suggestion that fantasy 'floats free'. *A Chance Child* clearly involves fantasy, since, literally speaking, a small boy does not walk into the past, and factory children could not be helped by a ghost from the future. But it does not float free from reality; on the contrary, it is deeply rooted – as surely the best fiction of any kind, including fantasy, must always be – in the realities of the human heart and the human predicament.

6. *Young Winter's Tales* 7 (ed. M. R. Hodgkin, London, Macmillan, 1976).

Jill Paton Walsh

Jill Paton Walsh writes:

I am not one of those writers who were always at it from the age of two. I began when I was twenty-six, in a desperate frame of mind, trying to beat back the boredom of being trapped in a small house alone with a baby that could not yet talk. I wrote for children out of a combination of humility and ignorance. I did not feel I had anything special to offer other adults; but I had been teaching, and I reckoned I did know what children liked. I knew just when they would begin to fidget and look out of the window when one read them the classics; I thought I might manage to write something that would please children.

In mitigation of such errors I can only plead that I quickly learned my mistake; found very rapidly that knowing what would please and being able to master the making of it were very different things, and that nothing could be done without understanding 'story' or 'narrative' or 'plot', whatever it is called, the central mystery of literature. I had graduated in English at Oxford without ever giving narrative more than a cursory glance. Abashed at the typewriter, I returned to Aristotle, the first critic, and from a practical need the best, and began to learn my trade.

I write now for children out of wild ambition, having understood that they are the best audience for many things, but also the hardest. To reach their possibilities without stumbling over their limitations one pares one's subject to the bones of its simplicity; one must find the ultimate structure of what truth one is dealing in, one must have the world clear and bright in view. Not everything can be said for children; not everything can be explained to them. But once it is not clogged up by hesitation and pretension almost anything can be *told* to them as a story.

Now that I *have* understood how difficult a task I set myself, when I began to write for children, it seems to me, though daunting, endlessly fascinating: technically far more challenging than the adult novel, and unambiguously worth doing. I shall keep trying as long as I have my wits about me, and energy to try anything.

K. M. Peyton

Kathleen Peyton was born in 1929. She went to Wimbledon High School, studied art in Kingston-on-Thames and Manchester, and ran away from home to marry a freelance commercial artist. During the next few years she travelled to many parts of the world and held a variety of jobs. Her first published book, Sabre, the Horse from the Sea *(1948), was written when she was fifteen, and she followed this with a number of horse stories and adventure stories before Oxford University Press published* Windfall *in 1962. She received the Carnegie Medal for* The Edge of the Cloud *(1969), and the Guardian Award for all three books in the* Flambards *trilogy. Her more recent books include* The Right-Hand Man *(1977),* Prove Yourself a Hero *(1977) and* A Midsummer Night's Death *(1978). Mrs Peyton lives in Essex with her husband and their two daughters.*

Strictly speaking, there is no such person as K. M. Peyton. There is Kathleen Peyton, who has written several books, and there is Michael, her husband, who collaborated on some of the earlier ones. A former publisher did not like the look of 'by K. and M. Peyton' on a jacket or title page, and so K. M. Peyton was born. But today 'K. M. Peyton' means Kathleen.

Mrs Peyton had in fact written her first published novel when she was Kathleen Herald, aged fifteen; and even before that she had produced half a dozen unpublished manuscripts, spread over many exercise books. 'I have always had a book on the go since the age of nine,' she once said. She married at twenty-one, and spent much of the next years travelling widely and impecuniously with her husband. By the time she was thirty-two she had published three novels about horses, four adventure stories for boys which first appeared as serials in *Scout* magazine, and much miscellaneous material, including the ghosted memoirs of a dog-trainer. Then, deciding she could afford to write a book to please herself, she produced *Windfall*, a story of sea adventure which was somewhat longer and a good deal deeper than her earlier ones. Its publication by Oxford University Press in 1962 marked her immediate breakthrough to the front rank of 'quality' children's writers.

Windfall was the work of a mature person and experienced writer, and has many of the best Peyton qualities. Kathleen Peyton is a person of action, and a writer on themes of action. She has, among many other gifts, the unusual one of writing extremely well about *movement*: about the way people move with and through and against the elements, in boats, on horseback or the box of a coach, and – in the *Flambards* novels – in those frail, wind-buffeted early aircraft.

It is clear from every page of *Windfall* that the author knew from her own perilous experience what it was like to sail a fishing smack in winter off the Essex shores, as her hero Matt does in that book. First-class adventure stories are not too common today, and ones as good as *Windfall* are rare indeed. To criticize its villain, Beckett, as being a figure of unqualified evil seems to me to be mistaken. Stories of peril at sea call for elemental qualities in their human participants, as awesome precedents remind us. The psychological subtleties of the drawing-room are inappropriate when the ship is listing at forty-five degrees, the sea sweeping the decks, the hull all but invisible, the mizzenmast gone, and the rigging trailing in the sea 'like the hair of a drowning woman'.

But although a splendid story, *Windfall* is clearly pressing against the confines of its genre. Matt is a figure of what the author herself calls 'simple courage', entirely right for the hero of a sea story; yet she shows him in a longer perspective, as a lad assuming adult responsibility, as a member of a community, and in his relationship with the rich man's son, Francis. The nature and limitation of this relationship are accurately summed up in the closing chapter, in which both boys realize that a temporary friendship has run its course and that their ways have to part.

The next step seems – with benefit of hindsight – obvious: that the author should add to her next book the further dimensions of depth of character and social analysis. And Mrs Peyton did indeed move in this direction with *The Maplin Bird* (1964), a story about an orphaned brother and sister in mid-Victorian England, in which the sea and fishing-smacks again play an important but this time a less dominant role. *The Maplin Bird* also marks the appearance of the first heroine in Mrs Peyton's mature work. Matt in *Windfall* had a sister, Anne, who barely had a speaking part; but Emily in *The Maplin Bird* steals the story entirely from her brother Toby. She.is resourceful, spirited and enduring; and she matures in the course of the action. The story has a limited happy ending; Emily's love for the gentleman-smuggler Adam Seymour brings her only pain, but she and brother Toby finish up with a cottage of their own, and freedom.

The Plan for Birdsmarsh (1965) was the first of Mrs Peyton's mature novels to have a contemporary setting. Birdsmarsh is a sleepy Essex village faced with the threat (or promise, depending on one's point of view) of development with a marina, hotel, swimming-pool, giant car park and the rest. Dreamy, un-boaty Paul hates the thought of it, but his friend Gus, a local working lad, can see the advantages. The resulting story is interwoven with a virtually separate one about a lifesaving suit invented by Paul's elder brother Chris, and about the trapping of a pair of industrial spies. The difficulty is not merely one of working two plots together; it is that the two plots belong to different kinds of book, an exploration of personal and social conflicts and an adventure story. The natural pace and the kinds of character required are not the same for both types of story. The result, to my mind, is an interesting failure, although the author has again extended her range, and Paul is more subtle than any of her previous heroes.

Thunder in the Sky (1966) went back in time to the start of the First World War, but was a big advance on *The Plan for Birds-marsh*. While the latter is complicated and somewhat uncoordinated, *Thunder in the Sky* has a more rewarding complexity. It can be read at more than one level. Sam Goodchild, at fifteen, works on the coastal sailing barges which have been switched at the start of the war to carrying freight and later ammunition to France. He cannot understand why his elder brother Gil, also on the barges, doesn't join the Army like any other young man. There is espionage in the air, and it looks as if Gil might be involved. Sam eavesdrops in a Calais bar, is caught, tied up, released, pursued out to sea, fired on; and so it continues until the climax in which Gil, who was indeed passing messages to the other side, sails his barge, loaded with explosives and on fire from a Zeppelin raid, away from the pier to a death that atones for everything.

At its face value this is what used to be called a rattling good yarn; and none the worse for that. Yet a reader who has passed beyond the stage of reading simply for plot and action will also find himself engaged with the morality and the pity of war, and with the ambiguous character of brother Gil. At a more mature level I do not think the book is quite complete. At this level it may appear that Gil is the true centre of interest rather than honest, innocent Sam, who is something of a throwback to the earlier brave but simple Peyton heroes. And one wants to know more about Gil; to see more of the background to his non-enlistment, his involvement in espionage, his suffering. We learn that he needs money to spend on a girl, and this may be explanation enough for younger readers, but, to cast a shadow of such length, Gil's love affair with faithless Agnes must be more than a mere plotting device. The author knows this and hints at it:

When Gil had got enough rum inside him, he called for Agnes Martin. George Young came to the door and told him to clear off, but Gil seized him by the collar of his smart white shirt, pulled him into the road and hit him. Agnes came out, saw George rolling in the dust and laughed. Then Gil told her to get her coat, and they went down the lane, their arms round each other, to where the tide was making silently over the shining mud, and the waders cried along the sea-wall.

We get only a glimpse or two of Agnes; she belongs to the 'other' book that the author did not write and probably never thought of writing, but that one feels to be present in a ghostly way behind *Thunder in the Sky*.

It is easy to suggest that the same book should 'work at all levels'; it is not easy and may often be impossible to meet this exacting demand. But the trilogy which began with *Flambards* in 1967 is complete and rounded-out while *Thunder in the Sky*, for all its merits, is not. Of all Kathleen Peyton's work, this trilogy still seems to me to be the most satisfying as well as the most substantial.

Flambards is the name of the decrepit country house to which the heroine Christina is sent at the start of the first book to live with her crippled, violent Uncle Russell and his two sons. The family fortunes, undermined by Uncle's expensive passion for horses and hunting, are in a desperate state; and Christina, who will be rich when she comes of age, suspects that she is meant to restore them by marrying Mark, the elder son. Mark, handsome and arrogant, shares his father's obsession with hunting. Will, the gentle younger brother, hates and fears riding and longs to fly aeroplanes, those flimsy, precarious things that are just starting to rise above the hedgerows. Then there is Dick, the groom, who teaches Christina to ride, and is kinder than anyone. All three love Christina in their various ways; but it is Will, the pioneer aviator, who carries her off from the dying house in the first book's final chapter.

The changing relationships of people are seen within a framework which itself is changing: sinking squirearchy and rising technocracy, old and new attitudes, class barriers that are still strong but showing the first cracks. It is a book of conflicts, extending right into the personality of the heroine; for Christina has something of the hard-riding Russells in herself, even though in the end she makes her firm choice of new against old, person against place or position, the gentle against the ruthless. It is a book of action in the exterior sense, too: there are vivid scenes of hunting, of early motoring and flying, of personal violence. (Uncle Russell's beating of Will for disobedience and

K. M. Peyton

Dick's beating-up of Mark for making his sister pregnant are both disturbingly powerful.)

The second and third books of the trilogy – *The Edge of the Cloud* and *Flambards in Summer*, both published in 1969 – satisfactorily complete the design, although they do not add to the stature which *Flambards* has established. The former is largely about Will's career as an aviator in the years immediately before the First World War. It is seen from the point of view of Christina, who fears for him with good cause, and suffers daily on his account. As a book on its own, *The Edge of the Cloud* is concerned with the tensions of a relationship overshadowed by danger and by a sense of impermanence. It stands somewhat apart from the other two books of the trilogy, which are centred on the house itself.

Possibly indeed the Flambards saga is really a two-part story, with the middle book as a prolonged interlude. In the third book we are back at Flambards. Uncle Russell has died; Will has been killed in the war and his brother Mark is reported missing. Christina, who has now come into her money, returns to the rundown house to pick up the pieces, to bear Will's posthumous child, to work the home farm. 'Flambards,' she has said to the house near the end of the first book, 'you are dying.' The theme of *Flambards in Summer* is rebirth, not only of the house but of the little community that belongs to it and that now takes a new form. And it is Christina who gives life, in all senses of the phrase. She is a heroine on the grand scale for a modern novel: determined, undaunted and above all strong – stronger by far than the men in her life.

Between the publication of the *Flambards* trilogy and the time of writing, a large part of Kathleen Peyton's work has consisted of a linked group of novels about Ruth Hollis (first seen in *Fly-by-Night*, published in 1968, as an eleven-year-old girl with a desperate longing to own a horse) and Patrick Pennington, who first appeared, separately, in *Pennington's Seventeenth Summer* (1970; American title *Pennington's Last Term*). The two were brought together in *The Beethoven Medal* (1971), and, growing older, became lovers and were married in *Pennington's Heir*

(1973). *The Team* (1975) moved back into an earlier phase of Ruth's life, before her meeting with Pat, when she was still obsessed with horses.

The two books about Ruth-before-Pennington are really pony stories, and are quite slight – though good enough to lend some distinction to a genre which is in many ways non-literary. (Like fiction about, say, football, it appeals largely to readers whose primary interest is in the thing itself; I remember learning from a librarian that pony books were often taken out of her library by children who read little or nothing else, and came back all nuzzled and nibbled, as if the horses had been reading them too.) In *Fly-by-Night*, Ruth, who lives on a housing estate, precariously acquires a pony which she then, while lacking both money and expertise, has to keep and feed and train. There is plenty of that fascinating detail about snaffle-bits and girths and other appurtenances that so delights the enthusiasts; and there is substance behind it, too. Wanting an animal may be an obsession; actually owning one is a responsibility.

The Team moves Ruth farther into the world of the Pony Club; and the author observes with sympathy but also with a hint of ironic detachment the obsession of horsy people with their sport. She understands and can convey the fascination of it; can even get the thoroughly unhorsy, such as myself, to appreciate the almost-cosmic significance of the Area Trials. And her gift for sheer movement is at full stretch when with Ruth we are actually riding Toadhall Flax in filthy wet conditions in the cross-country; we can feel the pounding horse beneath us, the mud and spray splashing up in our face, the suspense of fence and ditch. The knitting together of the team for the trials – four teenagers, four ponies, under the management of formidable Mrs Meredith – is the matter of the story; and Kathleen Peyton characterizes her horses as effectively as her people.

Anxious, conscientious Ruth, low in self-esteem but immensely determined, has in her the steel of the true Peyton heroine. And it is totally appropriate that on growing out of the pony world she should become involved with Patrick Pennington. The author sums it up, with what could be conscious irony, in *The Beethoven Medal*: Ruth 'knew that a good part of Patrick's attraction for her was this difficult core. . . She had always been attracted by difficulties. Both her ponies had been difficult, not ready-schooled, well-mannered animals . . . but prickly, uncertain creatures with wild pasts.'

To say that Patrick Pennington is a prickly, uncertain creature with a wild past is to understate his general cussedness. In *Pennington's Seventeenth Summer,* the first book in which he appears, he is in his last reluctant term at the Beehive Secondary Modern. He is 'a fourteen-stone hulk of a boy, with shoulders on him like an all-in wrestler, and long reddish-brown hair curling over his collar', constantly clashing with his teachers, his parents and the adult world at large, to say nothing of a few fights with his contemporaries. 'Essentially a thug,' says his headmaster; but Pennington is an astonishingly talented thug, since he is a genius at the piano, a brilliant swimmer, and excellent also at soccer-playing, sailing and dancing.

Handsome, sulky, sexy, restless, gifted: Pennington looks like an updated version of a young girl's dream. The adult world detests him, but he holds out against it and usually triumphs. Reading the book, you not only believe in him, you are on his side, you cheer him all the way. Afterwards you realize that the cards have been artfully stacked: your sympathy has been enlisted for Pennington by making him unbelievably loathed and misunderstood at school, especially by his mean-minded form-master Soggy Marsh. His parents, who have after all kept him on for an extra year at school and had him taught the piano, are shown as nasty and neglectful; his school rival Smeeton is slimy and malicious; and Police Constable Mitchell is unrelentingly down on him. When it all ends with Pennington triumphant and Mr Marsh humiliated in public, one feels that the one-in-the-eye delivered to Authority is possibly one-below-the-belt. Is Pennington likeable or even credible? Yes, I think he is – just – but he is a mass of contradictions, held together by the creative energy of the author.

In the second book about Pennington – *The Beethoven Medal*

– we see Ruth in the throes of desperate adolescent love for him; and no bones are made about why she finds him more attractive than the well-behaved boys her parents prefer. 'Loads of sex appeal,' her brother Ted explains to her mother. It is hard not to see this book and its successor *Pennington's Heir* as the breaking-in of Pennington by Ruth. At the end of the latter novel, Pennington is a reasonably responsible young husband and father, a concert pianist on the brink of a successful career. And he is a shadow of his old self. Whether he has simply grown up, as young men do, or has been tamed by Ruth is doubtful; in either case, he has become less interesting. An incident near the end of *Pennington's Heir*, in which he defends his virtue in a manner which would have done credit to Richardson's Pamela, is as embarrassing as it is unconvincing.

Kathleen Peyton is a prolific writer, and in the last year before the present study – 1977 – she had two novels out. *The Right-Hand Man* is set in the days of the stage-coach, and has a dashing young coachman as hero, a dying nobleman as his patron, an outrageous wager, villainy on the open road, a fight to the finish with bare fists, murder, perjury, a spell in Newgate Gaol and any amount of period colour. *Prove Yourself a Hero* links up with the Ruth books, in that the central figure, Jonathan Meredith, also appears in *The Team*. Jonathan, a member of a well-to-do family, is kidnapped and ransomed; he believes he behaved in a cowardly way during his imprisonment, and has to prove himself to himself and to his formidable mother. Neither of these, I think, is in the front rank of Mrs Peyton's work. Her best book since the *Flambards* trio is probably *A Pattern of Roses*, which appeared in 1972.

This is the only one of her books to have a fantasy element – though the fantasy is frail and ghostly, and conceivably is 'all in the mind'. Tim Ingram finds some hidden drawings, bearing his own initials, in the old cottage which forms part of his parents' newly acquired and converted country home. He feels an affinity with – seems, indeed, actually to see and hear – Tom Inskip, the farm lad who made the drawings and who died more than sixty years before. The story moves between 'then' and 'now'; we see Tom at key points in his short life, and we also see Tim with his no-nonsense friend Rebecca, trying to discover the truth about Tom. In the end, Tom's friendly ghost – if he *is* a ghost – saves Tim from disaster; saves him too, it seems, both from apathy and from being dragged by his father into the advertising rat-race.

Does Tom 'really' appear to present-day Tim? It is hard to say. On the one hand, Tim knows he has heard music from the past and that 'something in him was on the same wavelength as something that had happened before. He kept brushing against it, just occasionally. . .' On the other hand, towards the end, when Tim is sure that Tom will not come back any more, he 'felt as if a part of himself was missing. Tom *was* himself. Had he ever really been a ghost, or merely his – Tim's – own imagination? Some things had no answers.' Writers are not, of course, under obligation to supply all the answers. The ambiguity here was no doubt fully intended, and leaves a resonance in the reader's mind which would be lost if it were resolved.

The haunting quality of the novel owes much to this resonance, and much also to the figure of Tom, the poor boy from before the First World War with talent but without prospects. And Tom's relationships with Miss May, who wants to teach him, and with Netty, the Rector's niece who flirts lightly with him and gets him sacked from his job, are drawn with delicate precision. Tom is in love with Netty, but he 'knew that Netty wasn't kind. She was all sorts of other marvellous things, but she wasn't kind.'

It is strange that Kathleen Peyton, who can create wholly individual people, situations and relationships, is so often content with conventional ones which might have been borrowed from a class of fiction much inferior to her own. The gentleman-smuggler Adam in *The Maplin Bird* and the handsome cad Mark in *Flambards* could have stepped out of standard romantic novels. The same might be said of one or two of her heroes. Pennington – at least in the two later books about him – suggests fiction rather than life; so indeed does handsome Ned in *The Right-Hand Man*. Other masculine characters, like Matt in *Windfall*, Sam in *Thunder in the Sky*, and Dick in the *Flambards* books, are simple, brave and slightly wooden. She is better with the girls. Emily in *The Maplin Bird* and Christina in *Flambards* are splendid heroines, though they are, as she says herself, 'more or less the same person'; and Ruth, in the horse stories and Pennington books, while she has less in her of the spirited young lady, has a cousinship of determination with them both. There is something rather formidable about Peyton heroines. The last thing they would ever be is girlish.

Mrs Peyton can deal with large themes, and construct excellent plots if she is so minded. She can tell a story with great pace and certainty. In her historical or semi-historical novels her research appears impeccable, but she never gives the impression of bookishness; she knows in her fingers how to handle a boat or a horse, and one feels she would manage quite well in an ancient aeroplane. She has extended her territory book by book, and undoubtedly will extend it further. And there is one vital moment that occurs sooner or later in the best of her novels and accounts for much of their depth and strength: the moment of rejoicing at simply being here, to love and suffer and take what comes.

K. M. Peyton

K. M. Peyton writes:

Books are born in different ways. Some – most – evolve over a long period of time, ticking away at the back of the mind, the characters gradually taking shape, the sequence of events slowly forming. Others, strangely, come complete in a few days, ready-made books, sparked off invariably by one place or incident. This only happens to me when I am on holiday in unfamiliar surroundings. A yacht-launching at Mylor gave me the idea for *Prove Yourself a Hero*, the story worked out in my head in three days; and recently a canal cruise through Brittany produced in one mere day (a record!) a very tight, classic, hopefully perfect story, complete with characters, a bargain package. . .

But while this is going on, in my mind stewing away, bubbling, occasionally cooling, but irrevocably cooking, there is a great tangle of a book which occupies me continually, but will not fit into any accepted shape. It is a book about children, but not a children's book. It started life as two quite separate books, about two separate lots of people; then I had the idea of running the stories together and fitting them into one lot of people. A stunning idea, but creating terrible pitfalls. I can't get it right. There is no end to the thinking.

Meanwhile, I write an easy one, having actually asked my editor what he would like. He told me. Incredibly uncomplicated. The idea comes the same evening, involving some totally enjoyable 'research' over the summer holidays, trailing a group of children to tetrathlon competitions and getting worked up over Ali's fifteen-hundred-metre run and Jeremy's fantastic swim; sitting on the sea-wall cooking bangers over a barbecue while the scorers tot up points and the parents start packing up the wet towels and lemonade bottles. They laugh when I say I am working.

But they don't see the other side of the coin, and the disasters which never see the light of day, like the book I actually took back in a flurry of panic after it had been accepted for publication, and consigned to the scrapheap. The peace of mind that came from that impulsive decision was immeasurable.

177

A Sounding of Storytellers

I am very fortunate to get ideas so easily, but perhaps it is my misfortune too, that I am in such a hurry to tumble them out – and I do enjoy tumbling them out – that they suffer from a lack of dispassionate coolness on the part of their author. I am not a keen rewriter, but know that much could be improved if reconsidered at a later date. But by the later date I am too much involved in the next to go back.

I seem to have come to a stage where my books will have to divide between children's books and others. I have always said I would never write others, but now I feel I should, or else I shall be bending my material to fit where it does not belong. It has taken me a long time to reach this point, a case of a slow developer – or perhaps a sensibly nervous lack of confidence. The dividing line is so smudged, perhaps I can drift through it unawares. Or not. Time will tell.

Ivan Southall

Ivan Southall was born in Melbourne in 1921. His early ambition was to be a journalist, and his first articles and short stories were published when he was sixteen. In the Second World War he became a pilot in the Royal Australian Air Force and eventually captained a Sunderland flying boat. He was awarded the Distinguished Flying Cross for an action in which a U-boat was destroyed. After the war, he spent two years in London and then returned to Australia to become a freelance writer. He is married and has four children. Among Ivan Southall's books for young readers are Hills End *(1962),* Finn's Folly *(1969),* Matt and Jo *(1974) and* What About Tomorrow *(1977). He was awarded the Carnegie Medal for* Josh *(1971), and he has won the Australian Children's Book Council Book of the Year Award no fewer than five times.*

For more than a decade, Ivan Southall wrote adventure stories for boys about Squadron Leader Simon Black of the Royal Australian Air Force. Simon was, in the words of his creator, 'a decorated Air Force officer, a former flying-boat pilot who had flown in the Battle of the Atlantic, brown-eyed, black-haired, lean, six feet tall, Australian, modest, incredibly good, incredibly clever, incredibly brave, incredibly handsome – me. The super me. Same person, of course, as the super you.'[1] The Simon Black books were based, as Southall has acknowledged, on a conventional and stereotyped view of the nature of heroism and of the kind of action appropriate to a children's book. The day came when the thought of writing one more word

1. Ivan Southall, 'Real Adventure Belongs to Us', May Hill Arbuthnot Lecture 1974, *Top of the News*, June 1974, reprinted in *A Journey of Discovery* (Kestrel, 1975), pp. 66–93.

about his super-hero was more than he could stomach. Instead Southall sat down and wrote a novel about a group of ordinary, unheroic, flesh-and-blood children of the kind he himself knew.

Cut off by storm and flood in a little town in the mountains, miles from anywhere, with no parents around, these children faced catastrophe not with the aplomb of a fictional Air Force officer but with a lifelike mixture of bravery and cowardice, sense and silliness, cooperation and confusion. And, precariously but credibly, they blundered through. The book was *Hills End*, published in 1962. It was immediately successful, in the United States and Britain as well as Australia. This book and its successor *Ash Road*, written in 1965 and published in 1966, marked a new beginning in Ivan Southall's career as a professional writer. He pointed out in his Arbuthnot Lecture in 1974:

Real adventure cannot happen to super-heroes; by nature super-heroes would have to be insensitive to it; real adventure belongs to us. Being ordinary and inept are acceptable qualities, they give meaning to achievement. There must be contrasts within oneself. One must know weakness to know strength. One must be foolish to be wise. One must be scared to be brave. Adventure is simply experience; the mistakes often meaning more than the successes.[2]

In 1970 it was possible to feel that Southall had still not entirely discarded the support of a tried formula. The four full-length novels that followed *Hills End* had strong similarities with it and with each other. *Ash Road* (1965), *To the Wild Sky* (1967), *Finn's Folly* (1969) and *Chinaman's Reef is Ours* (1970) were all about groups of youngsters faced with disasters which taxed their reserves of physical and moral courage to the uttermost. All had fairly large casts in which no one individual was picked out as hero or heroine, and in which the members were shown in turn in their changing relationships with each other and with events. A reader acquainted with, say, any two of these five books would have had little difficulty in attributing the other three to Southall, even if he had had nothing to go on

2. ibid.

but a plot summary. A parody might well have been written under the title *Tether's End*.

Then came a change of direction. A group of later books – most notably *Bread and Honey* (1970), *Josh* (1971) and *What About Tomorrow* (1977) – have concentrated on the joys and agonies of a single central character and have gone deeply down inside that person, using a technique increasingly close to stream-of-consciousness. All the Southall novels have been challenging, sometimes harrowing, and seeming almost to force a confrontation, to ask the reader how much he could take. Yet they have penetrated more and more towards the core of adolescence: the often-desperate business of growing up and trying to find out what you are growing up *for*; what you can do and whether life will allow you to do it. Though seldom a comfortable read, they have offered a real emotional experience to those who were ready for it.

The five full-length novels running from *Hills End* to *Chinaman's Reef* are cinematic in technique: the point of view roves around, camera-like, from one character or pair of characters to another. This is a method to be used with caution when the end-product is a book rather than a film, because for most people reading is not so compulsive as viewing; the attention is jolted and may be lost at each point where the narrative jumps from one character to another. But Southall is exceptionally skilful at holding the reader's interest at these junctures; exceptionally good, too, at managing a large cast and making a number of children all entirely different and all interesting. These five books all have strong external action. The major plot element in each case is a catastrophe: storm and flood in *Hills End*, bush fire in *Ash Road*, air crash in *To the Wild Sky*, road accident in *Finn's Folly*, invasion of a town by a mining company in *Chinaman's Reef*. In later novels the action is less spectacular: the important events are those that take place in people's minds; but the books are no less powerful or disturbing. The intensity of personal experience makes up for any lack of obviously-exciting incident.

Hills End is almost a perfect novel of its kind. Although only one adult can be said to play a major role, the feeling of the whole community, adults as well as children, is strong from the start, as indeed it must be in order to give full weight to the blow that falls upon it. The rapid character-development and self-discovery of the children under stress are notable. For instance, in a few days and a couple of hundred pages Adrian, the boss's son and 'king of the kids', discovers himself to be a physical coward and moves through deep self-disgust to find himself again as a resourceful organizer; and all this time he remains unmistakably the same boy. In *Ash Road* the scope is broader, a full cast of adults is introduced, and the account of the bush fire's progress is absorbing in itself; yet the fire is a long, long time in arriving, the tension has to be sustained through many anticipatory chapters, and there is a feeling that the author is straining to keep it up, that the characters are running around in too many circles.

To the Wild Sky is a problem novel: in a way the most baffling of Southall's books. Six children set off in a private plane on a weekend visit. The pilot dies suddenly of a heart attack; one of the boys manages to fly the machine but is prevented by dust-storms from trying to land it until many hours later when, carried by tail-winds for hundreds of miles beyond his destination, he makes a crash-landing on a remote shore. For the rest of the book the children are seeking in a disorganized way to survive; they have at the end the slight encouragement of making fire, but they have no water and virtually no food, and they have found no signs of current human life. We do not know what happens to them.

It seems to me that this book presents the first two acts of a three-act drama. The first act is the flight and the second is the children's stranding and their attempt to sort themselves out. But what of the final act? Is it rescue, or is it – as seen in a premonition by one of the girls – death, slow and dreadful, one at a time? The author has left the last act to be written in the mind of the reader, and the few clues he offers are, to my mind, indecisive. But is it legitimate, artistically, to leave the story to be finished by the reader? In this case at least, I do not think it is.

The significance of the first two acts depends to a large extent on the third. If the children are doomed, they are not the same children as if they survive; the meaning of the story, and of their lives, is different. The ambiguity is too profound to be left unresolved. This seems to me to be the real difficulty of *To the Wild Sky*. Comparisons with William Golding's *Lord of the Flies* are of little relevance. The point of *Lord of the Flies*, as I understand it, is that the castaway boys regress towards savagery. That does not happen, and does not seem likely to happen, in *To the Wild Sky*; in fact, part of the problem faced by these children is that they are too civilized to cope.

Finn's Folly is an equally disturbing book. A crash at night on a hairpin bend in frost and fog; the parents of four children dead in their car; the driver of a lorry dying in his cab with his young daughter beside him; drums of deadly cyanide strewn around a hillside with a reservoir below; a mentally-retarded boy at large; and somewhere in the background the curse of a disastrous marriage still working itself out: it is hard to imagine a more harrowing set of circumstances. At the heart of the story is the brief love that springs up between fifteen-year-old Max and fourteen-year-old Alison, both just orphaned. Alison is still trapped in the cab of the truck beside her dead father.

There was a soft laugh, unlike any other he had ever heard, and he knew that it was a very special sound: the first laugh of a girl for a boy. It could never happen again, not the same sound or the same excitement that it stirred. He laughed also, as quietly as she had, and said 'Gee, Alison. . .' He went quiet then and was confused.

It is unlikely that a boy and girl would talk love in the midst of death and continuing crisis, but it is not impossible, for human nature is infinitely strange. And it is possible that their talk of love in these circumstances would not be callous or offensive. It seems that girl and boy are taking the places of lost mother and lost father for each other; and it could be that there is a deeper significance still, for here at the moment of death is the rebirth of love. If the author can make the incident credible in fact and acceptable in feeling, then objections must be withdrawn. But this is an exceedingly difficult task. I do not think it is accomplished. The trouble perhaps is that the pile-up of agony has been too great; the paradox is too extreme and deliberate. The power of belief will not stretch far enough and, in the absence of belief, the question of moral and emotional acceptability has no substance.

The action of *Finn's Folly* takes place within a night, and that of *Chinaman's Reef* within a day. A handful of families in an almost-ghost town 'built beside a copper-mine out in the middle of nowhere, Australia' faces the sudden arrival of 'a mammoth convoy of prime movers, trailers, bulldozers, caravans – all the might of the Pan Pacific Mining Company advancing like an invading army'. The company has bought up the town's leases and intends to demolish it and dig out what still lies underneath. The main characters are four local teenagers, their parents, and the man who heads the mining company's operation. With the invasion comes first a shattering eruption of all the issues that have stayed buried in the sanded-up life of the little community; then a panic in which everyone seems to be at cross-purposes; then the clash of attackers and attacked. The men drive off to seek support from the shire authorities, so it is the women and children who bear the heat of the day. And at the end of it all, the invaders prevail.

This is the kind of conflict that might be expected to stretch over weeks or months rather than be fought and finished in a day. One has a slight sense of artificiality; it seems that everything has been whipped up into one brief rush of events, as if the author were trying to impose on human actions the character of a natural catastrophe. There are advantages in the situation, however, since human conflict has possibilities that do not exist in fire or flood, in air or road crash. There is no arguing with *those*. The threat to Chinaman's Reef has its universal aspect – the quiet backwater finding itself in the way of material progress – and at one moment there is a glimpse of that progress in a horrifying, almost science-fictional aspect:

Ivan Southall

Cherry drooped at her mother's window, looking out on a shuddering world where not a man moved on foot, where there was not a human face except behind windscreen glass. There they presided, dimly seen, not like living men, but like figures of wax that might eerily stir on command. Cherry leaned there and cried a little and felt a million years alone. Vehicles obstructed her view but allowed anguished glimpses of a yellow-painted monster nervily squirting black puffs of smoke and thrusting itself about in jerks and stabs in an ill-tempered way, each thrust bearing behind it thirty tons of steel.

Whatever its faults, this is a searching novel. One's instinctive sympathy is with the resistance to invasion; but does Chinaman's Reef – this 'heap of sticks and stones' – deserve to live? Is not life in such a neglected unlovely place a desolating waste of years? What future can it hold for the young people? There is plenty here to think about.

Though the full-length novels carry more weight, two books which are closer to being long short stories seem to me to be among Southall's more successful work for children. These are *The Fox Hole* (1967) and *Let the Balloon Go* (1968). In *The Fox Hole*, a boy called Ken is trapped in a shaft which may be that of a long-lost gold mine, and his uncle, setting out to rescue him, is deflected by the prospect of sudden wealth. The book's approach to the sinister lure of gold recalls Scott O'Dell's *The King's Fifth*,[3] and is a reminder by contrast of the moral absence-of-mind which can so easily characterize fictional treasure-hunts. *Let the Balloon Go* is a terse, memorable tale about a spastic boy inside whom an active, adventurous one is signalling desperately to get out. Reluctantly left at home for once by his anxious mother, John climbs to the top of an eighty-foot tree.

It was everything he had longed for and never known. All words fell away, all demands that others should see him meant nothing any more. The bough swayed and he swayed with it; wind was like a cool sea against him; motion and wind together were a great calm that healed every pain he had ever known.

3. *The King's Fifth* (Houghton Mifflin, 1966; Longman, 1967).

'A balloon is not a balloon until you cut the string and let it go': that is what the book is about. At the top of the tree, John 'was strong. He was free. He was a boy like any other boy.' All that remains is that he should get safely down again; and until he does, the realization of his dream has – for the reader at least – an element of nightmare.

Let the Balloon Go may be seen as a forerunner of the later group of Southall novels in which fierce intensity and high pressure are concentrated on the experience of a single character. The protagonist of *Bread and Honey* is lonely thirteen-year-old Michael. The action takes place on Anzac Day, the public holiday when Australians commemorate their part in two world wars. Michael misses seeing the Anzac Day parade in his town; encounters on the beach the strange wide-eyed nine-year-old Margaret, who lives in an imaginative world of her own; and in her company meets the local bully and thrashes the bully's henchman. That is virtually all that happens; on the face of things it is a slight enough story. But Michael's day is full of stress and full of significance. The author himself has described *Bread and Honey* as 'the story of a boy's emotional awakening', and has said that he recalled it for rewriting because in the first version 'I had been afraid to face the sexuality of it.'[4] The sexuality of *Bread and Honey* has in fact caused a queasiness in some adult readers which I find understandable. Michael feels physical interest in this child of nine:

> For the first time in his life he saw the face of a girl as something he wanted to touch, and saw his hand go out to her as if it were part of someone else . . . he was the one who wanted to cuddle up and do the kissing to find out what it would be like. She was terrific, but so little, so young. It wasn't right.

In terms of children's fiction, this is not normal behaviour. Indeed, observation suggests that in life itself adolescent boys find little girls a nuisance – as Michael does at first with Mar-

4. Ivan Southall, 'Journeys of Discovery', *Australian Book Review*, July 1969, expanded in *A Journey of Discovery* (Kestrel, 1975), pp. 9–16.

garet – and that their early sexual interest tends, mercifully, to be in girls who are at least as mature as themselves. And where sexual attraction between young people occurs elsewhere in the later Southall novels – as it does in *Josh, Matt and Jo* (1974) and *What About Tomorrow* – it does not involve pre-teenage children.

Michael of course is one individual character, and must be accepted or rejected according to whether the author makes him credible rather than according to his conformity with accepted fictional behaviour. In fact his relationship with Margaret is innocent and is handled with great delicacy. But it is not surprising that some adults have found it disturbing; and a recurrent preoccupation with nakedness may also give rise to unease. Michael has been in trouble with a censorious neighbour for rolling naked in the grass, and has lost his best friend after the friend found him swimming naked at night; and there is embarrassed discussion between him and Margaret when she wants to take her clothes off and says she doesn't mind if he takes his off, too. There is also a question of whether the bathroom door at home should be locked. Nakedness has strong sexual connotations, and the subject does seem to come up rather frequently. It should be pointed out, however, that another issue is involved in these incidents: that of what is 'natural' and what is stuffily conventional.

Bread and Honey has other concerns. Michael's father is a scientist of extremely literal mind: 'What is Heaven but a question? All I know, Michael, all I can stake my life on, is that the earth is solid, the seas are liquid and the air is gas.' One supposes that in Margaret, who claims that she can travel with a magic ring and turn herself into an animal, Michael is encountering the world of the imagination. And the day itself is important. The ethics of war are in question. Is it the glory or the horror that is to be remembered, the honour or the shame? Or is the aim of Anzac Day to pretend that people don't forget? On Margaret's behalf Michael resists aggression (that is his own phrase) in standing up to the bullies; but 'did she know that he had fought for her? Did she care? Was this the way it was with wars?' and so on through a series of unanswered questions. *Bread and Honey* is a close-textured book with a great deal in it, and perhaps it is unfair to complain that it does not really get anywhere with the issues it raises. We cannot expect an answer for every question.

Josh, which won the Carnegie Medal, is an agonizingly concentrated piece of work. The distance between author and central character seems here to have shrunk to nothing. The actual story one takes to be fictional, though there are people, places and incidents which Southall has related to his own early days. Josh Plowman, highly-strung city boy who writes poetry, goes on a visit to his Aunt Clara Plowman at Ryan Creek, where his great-grandfather was an important personage and Aunt Clara is still held in some awe. At once he falls foul of the Ryan Creek youngsters whose values are different, who can't see why anyone should be squeamish about trapping a rabbit, and who have a good deal of latent resentment against an incomer, especially one who bears a well-known name and is thought likely to put on airs. Surviving his instant unpopularity and even physical assault, Josh proves his integrity and perhaps brings on a useful catharsis for Ryan's Creek, but he and the locals are still on separate planes and there is no real communication. He leaves to walk a hundred miles home to Melbourne, alone.

The stream of consciousness is here intensified to a nightmarish degree, and at times the use of present participles – a brilliant variation on the more commonplace use of the present indicative – gives the reader an almost unbearable sense of being right there in the middle of things:

Josh . . . in dire danger of being kicked senseless, trying to crawl for safety through a milling mob of cricketers. Fists flying everywhere. Kids running riot in astonishing numbers . . . kids pouring down the back road from the High Street, leaping off their bicycles and two-wheeled scooters, wheels in the air spinning, kids racing along the track below the railway embankment yelling like Indians and rushing into it, car brakes squealing, girls and grown-ups and shrilling women. Josh lying prostrate on his belly in the open, bottom uppermost, wailing for a bit of privacy. Fights raging yards out in the water, kids swimming for the trestles, pursuers after them, a man in umpire's clothing cracking heads together and yelling madly for order, schoolmaster Cotton wading in from another direction looking like Samson and sending kids flying, standing over Josh a leg to each side of him, dropping his black silk coat to cover him. Standing up there above him shouting hoarsely, 'Stop it. Stop it. Stop it. Stop it.'

The taste first left in the mouth by *Josh* is one of sourness and alienation. But time and thought may help one to discern a less bitter flavour. The children of Ryan Creek are earthy, they're a different breed from Josh, but they're not bad, they respect him in the end; they love Aunt Clara and she loves them. And Josh knows who he is. When he walks away it is not a defeat and he is not downhearted.

Josh waving each time until she [Aunt Clara] was gone from view.
But sky and yellow stubble, golden yellow plain, singing in the sun, kicking up his heels; brother, it can even rain.
Go away, crows. Find yourselves a body that's had its day. I'm walking mine to Melbourne town and living every mile.

Matt and Jo can be summed up with perfect adequacy as 'Boy Meets Girl': not a new subject but an inexhaustible one. Unfortunately the book is a disappointment. This time there are parallel streams of consciousness – boy stream and girl stream – which are stylistically remarkably alike. The brittle stridency, the jumpiness, the sheer noise of the words used are too much for the subject-matter. '"Fifty thousand volts, Jo, charging back and forth." "The lights in your eyes, Matt, blinding me half to death."' One doesn't believe it really felt like that. Even adolescents on the day of mutual discovery don't batter so hard on each other's senses and sensibilities as might be gathered from *Matt and Jo*.

What About Tomorrow?, however, is surely one of Ivan Southall's major achievements. The year is 1931. Fourteen-year-old Sam collides with a tram while delivering newspapers, and loses his bike and eight shillings' worth of *Heralds*. Disaster. No bike means no job. How can his hard-pressed family go on supporting him? Sam runs away; and most of the book describes his journeyings over the next few days, in which he suffers some hardship and anguish, gets casual help from several people, and falls in love with three different girls in quick succession. Interspersed with this account are short forward flashes to the Second World War, with Sam a flying-boat captain on what looks like his last, fatal mission.

The journey of the young Sam, it seems fair to say, is a microcosm of growing up; and death in war is what he is growing towards. At one point Sam the pilot looks back on Sam the fourteen-year-old: 'So then you were a boy with a man's job to do. Growing up if you're a boy is a man's job at any time. But dying's the job for now, and that's just got to be the job for a full-grown man.' There is an ingenious confluence of the book's two streams when it becomes clear that Mary, the last of the three girls encountered by young Sam, is the one the mature Sam has gone back to and married, till death them do part. His last words are addressed to her:

"Oh, Mary," Sam cried, "I have to leave you behind."
"Oh, Mary," Sam cried, "till I die."

Once again, this is a strongly personal book. It is hard to escape a sense of the futility of growing up to be killed. Yet it would be wrong, I think, to see this as a testament of despair. There is joy in it too, and though Sam's death is part of the tragedy of a generation there is at least the knowledge that he will have lived and loved and begotten a son.

Ivan Southall himself, like Sam, captained a flying-boat; and in *Fly West* (1974), a non-fiction book for young readers, he gives graphic accounts of missions over the wartime Atlantic. He has not however used the Second World War as a main subject or setting in his mature fiction for young people. This may well seem regrettable. Although by now there are several good books on the children's lists about various aspects of the war, there is none that comes near to being a masterpiece. Perhaps it is not possible for a single book or writer to get to the heart of something so vast as a world war. But in so far as any one person could do it, Southall surely is uniquely qualified to deal fictionally with the pity and terror, the power and the glory, the rightness and wrongness of it all.

It is no good, of course, telling writers what they should write, or lamenting what they have not written. The time comes when a man has had enough of his war. But in approaching the work that actually exists of a writer so deeply involved as Southall, it is proper and helpful to remember the intensity of his wartime experience. Sam, in *What About Tomorrow*, grew towards his death in action; his creator survived, but the book alone would be proof enough of his awareness ever since that survival was a privilege haphazardly bestowed. Ivan Southall would wish to be thought of as a writer, not as a war hero; but even as a writer he remains, crucially, the young man, three parts pacifist, who had never thrown a fist in anger, for whom 'fear was part of every day'; the young man who flew many perilous missions over the Atlantic, and completed his tour.

A Sounding of Storytellers

In the course of an article in the *Horn Book* for June 1968, Ivan Southall wrote:

I woke up one morning in 1960, thirty-nine years of age, determined never to write another book for children. The dear little darlings could go jump in the lake. The thought of producing one more word about my superhero [Simon Black of the Royal Australian Air Force] was more than I could stomach. The sense of relief, of escape, of freedom was bliss indeed.

At the time, I was considering a theme for a novel. I had never written a novel and had never pretended to be a creative writer in the strictest sense, but I was faced with a time delay before I could start in earnest my next documentary, which was to take me to the Woomera Rocket Range; and Woomera was not ready to receive me. As doubtfully endowed as I felt my talent for literary experiment to be, the theme for the novel began to look like the source of a story that might involve children of the ordinary kind. But I had, after all, sworn off children's books and with my Simon Black mentality had never peopled any book with flesh-and-blood average folk, adults or children. For children, I had produced superheroes; for adults, giants, all larger than life. If a subject had failed to attain heroic proportions he had failed also to hold my professional interest.

Now, for the first time, I found myself looking at my own children and their friends growing up round about me. In their lives interacting one upon the other at an unknown depth, I began to suspect with genuine astonishment that here lay an unlimited source of raw material far more exciting than the theme itself. Thus there came a positive moment of decision for me.

Hills End, one of the most exciting adventures of my life, physical or mental, poured out from the first word to last in six weeks, a fraction of the time I had devoted to anything else. Six to twelve months was the usual run. *Hills End* did not stick to plan and veered far from the predetermined plot; the characters dominated and directed its course. It surprised my fondly respected Australian publishers, not favourably at first. I had to defend it with spirit, and for various reasons publication was delayed for two years. This interminable time convinced me they were printing it only to please me, and discouragement sent me off in other directions. Not until June, 1964, was I free to look seriously at the surprising fact that *Hills End* possessed merit discernible to others and might indicate an area I should examine again . . .

Ash Road came, as *Hills End* had come, clearly and with elation, filled with the excitement of discovering the minds of children and of finding a degree of involvement worth every moment of the months of search. I felt that I had become a child again, that I was writing *out* of my own childhood, and that the standards of maturity were necessary only as a filter of the most superficial kind. *Ash Road* was a raising-up, not a writing-down. It was an appreciation of the vivid colour of childhood, of its heightened reality, of the tensions, impressions, perceptions, toughness and anxieties that the adult forgets and dismisses as ultimately unimportant. Heaven forbid that I should imply that these qualities infuse the book, but they were *my* reward, *my* dividends.

There was also the discovery that truth is more purely expressed through the medium of fiction than it is in works allegedly of fact. A critical discovery far from unique or profound, but something that each writer must learn from life for himself. Writing had always been a fulfilment, but never before, except with *Hills End*, in this particular way.

Hills End, I suppose, was a diversion; but *Ash Road* was the conscious if imperfect beginning of a different professional and private life.

Patricia Wrightson

Patricia Wrightson was born in Lismore, New South Wales, in 1921.
She received part of her education through the State Correspondence
School, which gives lessons by post to children who live in remote
places. For several years she worked in hospital management, and she
was editor of the New South Wales Department of Education's School
Magazine *from 1970 to 1975. She is divorced and has a grown-up son*
and daughter. Among her novels are 'I Own the Racecourse!'
(1968), The Nargun and the Stars *(1973) and* The Ice is Coming
(1977).

Patricia Wrightson published her first novel in 1955. She is not
prolific, and twelve years later she had produced only four more
books. By then she had built up a modest reputation as an
intelligent and perceptive regional writer, but outside Australia
her name was still not widely known. Then in 1968 came '*I
Own the Racecourse!*' (in America *A Racecourse for Andy*), a story
about a backward boy who 'buys' a city racetrack for three
dollars and insists on taking a share in running it. It was highly
successful, both with children and with adult reviewers, and
Mrs Wrightson was suddenly recognized far beyond her own
shores as a leading children's writer. In the ten years from '*I
Own the Racecourse!*' to the present she has added only three
more novels to her total, making nine in all over a period of
twenty-four years; but the three have shown a remarkable
extension of scope and have greatly increased her reputation.
There has been no slack in her development.

'*I Own the Racecourse!*' now seems to mark her farthest
advance in the direction indicated by her early work. *The
Crooked Snake* (1955) and *The Bunyip Hole* (1958) had shown a

talent for managing a cast of children, both as individuals and groups, and an unusually strong sense of place; her stories were, and continued to be, notable for the almost tangible solidity of their settings, whether in the bush, a little seaside resort, or the bustling and various city of Sydney. *The Rocks of Honey* (1960) had demonstrated exceptional imaginative range and a willingness to tackle large and difficult themes. *The Feather Star* (1962) was remarkable for the sensitivity and precision of its character-drawing and its grasp of the ways in which children change as they grow up, while *Down to Earth* (1965) gave play to a bold comic imagination and a gift for making ideas interesting. All these qualities came together in '*I Own the Racecourse!*', which was one of the outstanding English-language children's books of its decade: a triumph in the mode of contemporary realism.

In the three books which have succeeded '*I Own the Racecourse!*', Mrs Wrightson has moved into the exacting field of fantasy. She does not underrate its difficulty. She looks on fantasy as an extremely serious mode: a form of writing that needs to be powerful rather than pretty. 'Fantasy,' she has said, 'is man thinking about reality but beyond the known facts. Its concern is with life, and its need is to convince.'[1] She abjures what she calls the Big Magics, the great creative myths which she regards as sacrosanct, unavailable to the modern writer, limited by their own authority. She sees the grass roots of fantasy in the traditional world of fairies, monsters and lesser magic. But she is convinced that in an Australian setting the traditional creatures of folktale from far-off countries are out of place. Instead she has introduced the folk-spirits of the Aborigines, inhabitants of an ancient land which is new only to its recent settlers. It can be seen with hindsight that *The Rocks of Honey* foreshadowed a later preoccupation with the land, its original People and their magic, and that *Down to Earth* was a

1. Patricia Wrightson, 'The Nature of Fantasy', paper delivered at the National Seminar on Children's Literature, Frankston State College, 1975, printed in *Readings in Children's Literature*, ed. Robinson (Frankston State College, 1977), pp. 220–43.

fantasy which could have been described as 'thinking about
reality but beyond the known facts'; but the nature and depth of
Mrs Wrightson's involvement with the themes underlying her
more recent books could not, I think, have been predicted.

Of the early books, *The Crooked Snake* and *The Bunyip Hole*,
after being out of print for several years, were brought back into
the lists in 1973 and have since been reprinted. *The Crooked
Snake* is about a group of boys and girls who form a secret
society, set out with cameras on a holiday project, and find
themselves in conflict with loutish older schoolfellows whom
they call the D.P.s, or Dangerous Persons. (Grown-ups are
Parents and Citizens.) In comparison with the author's later
work it seems unpretentious, almost naïve; the nice children
who form the society are right-minded and constructive,
reminding one slightly of Arthur Ransome's Swallows and
Amazons; the baddies are consistently nasty and are duly defeated in the end. *The Bunyip Hole* has a superficial similarity;
the Collins children, picnicking and camping beside a natural
pool which they wish to clear for summer use, are harried by a
couple of older boys they call the Ring-Tailed Bandicoots. But
here the most important happenings are those that take place
within the Collins family, and particularly inside young Binty,
a timid boy with too much imagination for his own comfort.
Binty sets out full of apprehension to rescue his dog Homer
from the Bandicoots, and finishes up trapped with Homer on a
ledge with a chasm beneath him; his rescue is due to his own
painfully-mustered courage as well as the efforts of his
resourceful older brother and sister.

Compared with these two, *The Rocks of Honey* is ambitious.
It begins in a matter-of-fact way, but goes on to open up some
unexpected perspectives. The main characters are a trio of
children: Barney, the practical son of a farmer; Eustace, an
amiable aboriginal boy who responds to every suggestion with
a cheerful 'I don't mind'; and Winnie, a disconcertingly silent,
independent and unpredictable small girl. The two boys
become engaged in a quest for an ancient stone axe, reputed to
lie hidden among the group of rocks now known as the Three

Patricia Wrightson

Sisters but formerly as the Rocks of Honey. It is a pleasantly casual quest, the excuse for a good deal of exploring and picnicking and den-making; and then the story suddenly takes off, with the interpolation of a chapter telling how, long years ago, Warrimai the club-thrower made the axe, and how he came to put it, with a curse upon it, among these rocks. And when the axe comes directly into the story, tension rises and persists.

In the midst of a storm, Winnie finds the axe. Eustace and his uncle, as aboriginals, are convinced that it should be put back where it came from. Barney thinks this is nonsense. But soon the axe is the cause of three strange accidents, one after the other. Perhaps they are only coincidence, but still . . . Barney and Winnie now agree that the axe should go back. And, replacing it among the Rocks of Honey, Eustace hears in the wind the Song of the Old King:

. . . Oh, my country, the warm land of the Honey,
  Have you broken and thrown away your own brown people?

The underlying theme, it becomes clear, is a weighty one: the changing relationship of the land and the two peoples. And the author has sought to indicate the different ways of thought and feeling of the brown people and the white. Between Barney and Eustace, who have never felt any racial antipathy, the quest for the axe brings a believable strangeness. The different moods of the story reflect a similar duality. In the second half there is nothing explicitly supernatural, but there is a pervading sense of old magic, an awareness that there could be more in heaven and earth than practical farmers' sons normally think of. *The Rocks of Honey* is not entirely successful; its transitions are sometimes awkward, and the author may have reached out for more than she could grasp at that stage of her development; but it is an impressive story, and comes to seem more so at a second and third reading.

The Feather Star has a familiar and apparently simple subject, though not an easy one to handle: the beginnings of a girl's growing up. Mrs Wrightson catches exactly the feeling, common in adolescence, of no longer knowing who or what one is.

197

On one occasion, fifteen-year-old Lindy, on holiday at the seaside, wanders along the beach and picks up shells:

Soon she had collected three pink, glittering shells, a delicate blue one, a twisty bit of driftwood like a snake, a fan-shaped sponge and a lump of pumice. She gathered them with the same small excitement with which she had gathered other hoards like this, year by year since she was tiny; and now, all at once, the excitement went out of them. What would she do with these things if she took them home? . . . She put them all down on a stone so that she could forget them without actually throwing them away, and went to sit on the rocks at the end of the wall.

With the girl who works in the shop – Felice, pronounced Fleece – and two boys, she forms a tentative foursome: shy, teasing, self-conscious, not knowing what to say to each other. The feather star of the title is a sea creature found by Lindy in a cave; broken, it will grow again two or threefold, and it symbolizes – one assumes – the breakup of childhood. Interestingly, Lindy's loss of childish innocence comes not in any of the obvious ways but through a series of encounters with a dreadful, censorious, all-hating old man. There is no reconciliation with him because he is lost, irredeemably lost, and the realization that this can happen is a fearful thing. 'She sobbed and sobbed, child and woman together, for the tragedy and wickedness of Abel. She sobbed for useless misery and bitterness; for age with its eyes on the ground refusing life, wasting all the adventure and beauty of a whirling planet in space.'

The 'adventure and beauty of a whirling planet in space' is something of which Mrs Wrightson is continually and significantly aware, and to which there are references at several places in her books. Add courage and humour and you have the main themes of *Down to Earth*, a strange fantasy set in the streets of Sydney and opened and closed by the arrival and departure of 'Martin the Martian'. It is not science fiction: it is in part a look at life here as it might seem to an intelligent visitor from another world – an idea which goes back at least to the Persian Letters of Montesquieu in the early eighteenth century, though Persia is no longer far enough away. Not only is there the question of how we look to an outside observer; there is the question of what we would *do* about such an observer if we became aware of him.

To George and Cathy, who find him living in an empty house, Martin looks like an ordinary boy. This is a mystery of perception which he tries to explain to them: 'To you I just look like an Earth person, because that's the only sort your brain can see.' Actually it is doubtful whether Martin is 'a boy' in his own society, or whether the idea would mean anything there; but George and Cathy look on him as a boy and feel protective towards him. And Martin needs protection, for, however intelligent, he is quite guileless, unequipped with the self-preservatory cunning that we all need to survive in the civilized jungle we inhabit. When he falls into the well-meaning hands of the Child Welfare Department, George and Cathy know they must rescue him and keep him out of the way of authority until he can catch a (space) ship back to wherever he came from. All in all, this is a slight but far from feeble story which pokes mildly satirical fun in several directions.

It also shows children taking responsibility on themselves for another child (or at least a being that looks like one). The sense of responsibility which children will accept – usually for younger or weaker children – is a recurrent Wrightson sub-theme, one that comes straight from life and that is not over-used in modern children's fiction. Joe and Mike, the friends of backward Andy in *'I Own the Racecourse!'*, care about him, stand up for him, and worry when everyone around him encourages his delusion that he's really bought the racecourse with the three dollars he paid to a tramp. 'He's getting in deeper all the time,' says Joe. 'He's got to come out of it.' Mike sees it differently: the episode is doing Andy a power of good, and since he is being humoured by the staff and generally treated as the owner, why then, for the present he *does* own the racecourse.

Whichever of them is right, the thing must end some time, for Andy cannot spend the rest of his life in a magnificent dream. There are practical reasons, too, why it has to stop; for Andy, though a mascot to the men, becomes an increasing nuisance to the racecourse's management. One wonders what way out there can be that will not deal a fearful psychological blow to Andy. But the author finds one; and it is the perfect and satisfying answer. A truly original plot is just about the rarest thing in fiction; '*I Own the Racecourse!*' has one.

As Mrs Wrightson asks, how real is reality? For that matter, what is ownership? The land and buildings of the racecourse are nothing; its true existence is only in action, especially when the trotting races are on in the great illuminated stadium:

With a rustling and drumming the horses sprang into view, spread wide across the track. Powerful, beating forelegs, deep, straining chests and rolling eyes, they hurtled along the track straight at the boys. The three of them hung silent and breathless on the rails with the crowd packed round them. The voice from the amplifiers chanted on. . . Cockaded heads high, the fierce horses passed. The drivers in their shining satin were perched above whirling wheels. The horses swung towards the inner rail and flowed in a dark stream round the curve. . .

Round the track again, and a string of red lights flashed as they passed the big stand. The amplified voice grew frenzied and was almost drowned by the roaring of the crowd. They went by like dark thunder, whips flashing and drivers' faces grim; and round the track the roar of the crowd travelled with them. This time a white light flashed, and the horses went flying separately, slowing and turning one by one. The race was over.

It is magnificent; and nobody can own it any more than Andy.

The three books which followed '*I Own the Racecourse!*' could all be grouped together under the title of the first of them, *An Older Kind of Magic* (1972). Important parts are played in all of them by those indigenous spirits of Australia which Patricia Wrightson has adopted and adapted. There are the Nyols, small and stone-grey, 'simple creatures, not very clever, but bright with the happy mischief of children', who invite all their visitors to wrestle with them; the Potkooroks, golden-eyed froglike tricksters of the streams and swamps; the wispy elusive Turongs in the trees: these and a great many more emerge in the course of the three books.

The use of Aboriginal folklore does not of course alter the fact that the novel is a sophisticated product of the Western culture in which Mrs Wrightson herself grew up: she has not actually created or re-created a native Australian form. But she has certainly tapped new sources and given an impressive new stimulus to her work. Each of the three novels is successively more ambitious; and the last, *The Ice is Coming* (1977), prompts and indeed appears to invite comparison with Tolkien or Le Guin.

The first of the three books contrasts this older, rooted form of magic with a cheap, shoddy modern kind, exemplified in big-business wizardry and the television commercial. The place is the city centre of Sydney, and the exact time is important: it is that of the return of a comet, last seen a thousand years ago and next to be seen a thousand years hence. It is a time that, fictionally, can be supposed to activate all potential sources of magic. The central thread of the story concerns the thwarting by children, with some supernatural aid, of a property speculator's plan to take over part of the Botanical Gardens for a car park; but to say that is not to give much idea of its real nature. Its view of the city is panoramic, or rather, layered. High in the sky is that comet; under it lie the rooftops (on one of which live Rupert and Selina, children of a Ministry caretaker); below them are the streets and public gardens of downtown Sydney; and lower still is the living rock in whose caverns and crevices the small grey shadowy Nyols survive.

There is a hierarchy of creatures, too: from the important Minister and the property man Sir Mortimer, through the T.V. commercial-maker Ernest Hawke and the ordinary families, down to dog, cat and kittens, 'pet' lizard and cockroach: all weave their way in and out of the story. The T.V. advertising man kills the car park project with a demonstration concocted from shop window models, brought briefly alive by a once-in-a-thousand-years magical stunt. But it is the older, more dangerous magic that stops Sir Mortimer in his tracks, literally. He is turned to stone. In spite of this last gruesome touch, *An Older Kind of Magic* is a light, easily-readable story. It should not be underrated; there is a great deal in it that is original and stimulating. But the Nyols, Potkooroks and other creatures seem clearly to be out of place in the centre of Sydney; they are more at home, more readily credible, in the less-populated settings of *The Nargun and the Stars* (1973) and *The Ice is Coming*.

The Nargun, in the first of these, is an ancient thing which looks at first sight like a huge rock but is, in its slow way, alive. It is dangerous, a stone beast of prey, but it is not evil; it is what it is.

Sometimes it remembered the world's making and cried for that long agony. Sometimes it felt anger: for a fallen tree, a dried-up pool, an intruder, or for hunger. Then too it cried. It had a sort of love: a response to the deep, slow rhythms of the earth; and when it felt the earth's crust swell to the pull of the moon it sometimes called in ecstasy. It had no fear; but a wide sunny place, or any strange thing, made it uneasy. Then it crouched in stony stillness and little lizards ran over it.

The principal people in this story are Simon, whose parents have been killed in a car crash, and his elderly distant-cousins Charlie and Edie, the matter-of-fact owners of a sheep run, who believe in the spirits for the perfectly good reason that they have met them. The Nargun, perched on the mountain high above Charlie's and Edie's house, is a menace; and, with the uncertain help of the Potkoorok in the nearby swamp, they and Simon deal with it. It is walled in by a rock-fall for ever; or almost for ever. We leave it waiting patiently 'for the mountain to crumble; for a river to break through; for time to wear away'. In this book the accurate-seeming topography, the quiet firmness of the telling, the total believability of the down-to-earth old couple, carry great conviction; there is something more truly spine-chilling here than anywhere else in Mrs Wrightson's work. (The turning of Sir Mortimer Wyvern to stone is a shock, but it is too sudden to terrify; and there is, in the context, something undignified and even a shade comic in his fate.)

Patricia Wrightson

In an author's note to *The Ice is Coming*, Patricia Wrightson remarks that she knows 'a country as powerful and as magical as Earthsea or Middle Earth. It is the only one I know and the one I want to write about.' It is of course Australia. The comparison is not one which an author would make lightly, since it can hardly avoid being extended from the countries to the books which are set in them. And although *The Ice is Coming* is not particularly long – 212 pages in the original hard-cover edition – it is a book of weight and substance, a major imaginative endeavour, whether successful or not.

The Ice is Coming begins by characterizing the population of Australia. There are the Happy Folk, who live in the cities and play on the beaches; there are the Inlanders, the old settlers; and there are the People, who 'are dark-skinned, with heavy brows and watching eyes, and they belong to the land; it flows into them through their feet'. And once again there are the spirits, of whom the People have known for a long time but said little. The Ninya are men of ice who live in frosty caverns under the fiery sand in the central desert, and who want to come out into the world, raise mountains of ice, bind up the rivers, and build the cold crystalline land they desire. The impediment is the Eldest Nargun, created in the molten beginning of things and holding the power of fire.

The Ninya can only have their way if they can clench a fist of ice upon the Eldest Nargun, now lying at the edge of the sea in the far South. They set off through the rocks to find it; and Wirrun, a young man of the People, learning of the patches of unexpected ice that mark their path, sets out overland to stop them. He is accompanied by the long frail female Mimi, borne by winds from the North, and he receives from Ko-in, protector of the land, a 'power of the people' which entitles him to help from spirits and creatures encountered along the way. His journey culminates in the discovery of the Eldest Nargun (there is a great surprise here which it would be wrong to disclose to readers who may not yet be acquainted with the book) and the defeat of the Ninya.

The story is on an epic scale, and is told in a style which is broadly appropriate (though Wirrun's own speech is a form of demotic English). It is a children's book to the extent to which *The Lord of the Rings* or *A Wizard of Earthsea* or *Watership Down* is a children's book. I should be very surprised, however, if it were to achieve the reputation or popularity of any of these titles. The trouble does not, I think, lie with the Australian setting or with the author's sense of it, which is admirable. And although, as I have indicated, the introduction of aboriginal folklore does not alter the fact that a novel is a sophisticated product of Western culture, that does not mean that it cannot be used successfully; on the contrary, it may well be that this is the only way to make an Australian epic fantasy viable. I suspect that what is lacking is something quite simple: the power of sheer compelling narrative. The story gives the impression of going on and on; it has its longueurs; it brings in more and more creatures, many of whom do not contribute anything very striking to the action; it builds up tension only occasionally, and then not for long. Disbelief is not always willingly suspended; one finds oneself asking why the Ninya should begin their campaign at this moment out of thousands of years, whether Wirrun would really have given up his job to embark on this unlikely-looking chase, and whether a few ice patches would be dramatic enough to create the stir they do. Possibly these are niggling complaints, not to be taken too seriously; but the fact that one is bothered by them may be an indication that the story does not have the speed and force that would brush such niceties aside. *The Ice is Coming* does not, I think, quite come off; it is not so good a book as *The Nargun and the Stars*. I offer this judgement with respect and with regret, with a willing acknowledgement that it is only the verdict of one person, and with the further thought that in any case one writer's failure may be much more interesting and valuable than another's success. Certainly the book does not diminish Mrs Wrightson's reputation. She remains an able, serious and courageous writer, with an invaluable readiness to attempt something new and difficult.

One does not expect the majority of children – or adults – to stop and think about the issues a story may raise. Most of us read fiction for pleasure, and there is nothing wrong with that. Yet the book that is exhausted on superficial reading is a bad one almost by definition, whereas a sense that there is more than meets the eye will often emerge half-consciously to enrich the experience of reading. One of the marks of a good novel is that it leaves one with the feeling that there is more to be discovered on further acquaintance. Patricia Wrightson has written several books of the kind that are worth coming back to, the kind that linger and echo in the reader's mind.

A Sounding of Storytellers

Patricia Wrightson writes:

My son, who shows no inclination to write and is quite unpretentious as a reader, has yet an uncanny perceptiveness of the craft of writing. He doesn't comment much or readily; you often have to dig. When the comment does come it is couched in his own terms and you may have to work them out. But the point, when you reach it, will be penetrating, diagnostic, and almost certainly right. Since he was eleven he has been the most trusted reader on my private panel.

So when he returned the manuscript of *The Nargun and the Stars* with the comment, 'You've been working up to this from the very beginning, haven't you?' I was startled but not quite incredulous; when I had time I thought. I went back over my own tracks – not a long way but each step keenly experienced. And yes: if you allow that I first had to learn to hold a pen, then each book at least from the second on was a move towards this kind of fantasy. Not the escape from life that some people see as fantasy, nor the symbolism of life that is some fantasy, but that strangeness and fullness of life that spills out of the bucket of reality – the human experience of fantasy. I found my footprints damp with it, and later my son pointed out the drips I had missed.

I'm not yet sure what this means. People have begun to regard me as a fantasy writer and maybe they are right; I just don't know. The trouble was that this kind of fantasy needs a wider reference than the symbolic kind. It needs to be rooted in the profound and primitive experience of folklore, and I had to discover (from an Australian writer's point of view) the folklore. When it was found, and found so rich and strong, the folklore made demands in its own right. When the trio of books is finished that began with *The Ice is Coming*, will the folklore be satisfied? Will I? I can't see ahead.

A cow is a restless and dissatisfied creature until it has broken into the closed field. After that it wants to break out again. I don't feel like a fantasy writer contentedly settled in the right field. But I suspect that any other kind of story will have to be demanding indeed, and rich in possibilities, to tempt me out of it.

A Note About the Author

A Note About the Author

John Rowe Townsend was born in Leeds and was educated at Leeds Grammar School and Emmanuel College, Cambridge. He worked as a journalist on the *Yorkshire Post* and the London *Evening Standard* before becoming a sub-editor and, later, art editor of the *Guardian*. He edited the weekly international edition of the *Guardian* from 1955 to 1969, and retained a connection with the paper as children's books editor until 1978.

John Rowe Townsend is himself a distinguished writer for young people, and his books include *Gumble's Yard* (1961), *Hell's Edge* (1963), *The Summer People* (1972), *Forest of the Night* (1974) and *The Xanadu Manuscript* (1977). His novel, *The Intruder*, received the *Boston Globe-Horn Book* Award in 1970 and won the Silver Pen award from the English Centre of International P.E.N. in the same year. He has also published two important books about children's literature, *Written for Children*[1] and *A Sense of Story*,[2] and he has written and lectured widely on the subject in both Great Britain and the United States. John Rowe Townsend now lives with his family in Cambridge, England.

1. *Written for Children* (Garnet Miller, 1965; revised ed., Kestrel, 1974; Lippincott, 1975).
2. *A Sense of Story* (Longman, 1971; Lippincott, 1971).

Author Bibliographies

The select bibliographies which follow list the principal children's books of each author, in order of publication. Both the British and American publishers of each title are cited, where appropriate, and the publisher in the country of origin is stated first.

Nina Bawden

THE SECRET PASSAGE. Gollancz, 1963; Lippincott, 1964, as THE HOUSE OF SECRETS.

ON THE RUN. Gollancz, 1964; Lippincott, 1965, as THREE ON THE RUN.

THE WHITE HORSE GANG. Gollancz, 1966; Lippincott, 1966.

THE WITCH'S DAUGHTER. Gollancz, 1966; Lippincott, 1966.

A HANDFUL OF THIEVES. Gollancz, 1967; Lippincott, 1967.

THE RUNAWAY SUMMER. Gollancz, 1969; Lippincott, 1969.

SQUIB. Gollancz, 1971; Lippincott, 1971.

CARRIE'S WAR. Gollancz, 1973; Lippincott, 1973.

THE PEPPERMINT PIG. Gollancz, 1975; Lippincott, 1975.

REBEL ON A ROCK. Gollancz, 1978; Lippincott, 1978.

Vera and Bill Cleaver

ELLEN GRAE. Lippincott, 1967.

LADY ELLEN GRAE. Lippincott, 1968.

WHERE THE LILIES BLOOM. Lippincott, 1969; Hamish Hamilton, 1970.

GROVER. Lippincott, 1970; Hamish Hamilton, 1971.

THE MIMOSA TREE. Lippincott, 1970; Oxford University Press, 1977.

THE MOCK REVOLT. Lippincott, 1971; Hamish Hamilton, 1972.

I WOULD RATHER BE A TURNIP. Lippincott, 1971; Hamish Hamilton, 1972.

DELPHA GREEN AND COMPANY. Lippincott, 1972; Collins, 1975.
ELLEN GRAE, AND LADY ELLEN GRAE. Hamish Hamilton, 1973.
ME TOO. Lippincott, 1973; Collins, 1975.
THE WHYS AND WHEREFORES OF LITTABELLE LEE. Atheneum, 1973; Hamish Hamilton, 1974.
DUST OF THE EARTH. Lippincott, 1975; Oxford University Press, 1977.
TRIAL VALLEY. Lippincott, 1977; Oxford University Press, 1977.
QUEEN OF HEARTS. Lippincott, 1978.

Peter Dickinson

THE WEATHERMONGER. Gollancz, 1968; Little, Brown, 1969.
HEARTSEASE. Gollancz, 1969; Little, Brown, 1969.
THE DEVIL'S CHILDREN. Gollancz, 1970; Little, Brown, 1970.
EMMA TUPPER'S DIARY. Gollancz, 1971; Little, Brown, 1971.
THE DANCING BEAR. Gollancz, 1972; Little, Brown, 1972.
THE IRON LION. Little, Brown, 1972; Allen & Unwin, 1973.
THE GIFT. Gollancz, 1973; Little, Brown, 1974.
CHANCE, LUCK AND DESTINY. Gollancz, 1975; Little, Brown, 1976.
PRESTO! HUMOROUS BITS AND PIECES (editor). Hutchinson, 1975.
THE BLUE HAWK. Gollancz, 1976; Little, Brown, 1976.
ANNERTON PIT. Gollancz, 1977; Little, Brown, 1977.
HEPZIBAH. Eel Pie, 1978.

Paula Fox

MAURICE'S ROOM. New York, Macmillan, 1966.
A LIKELY PLACE. New York, Macmillan, 1967; London, Macmillan, 1968.
HOW MANY MILES TO BABYLON? David White, 1967; London, Macmillan, 1967.
DEAR PROSPER. David White, 1968.
THE STONE-FACED BOY. Bradbury Press, 1968; London, Macmillan, 1969.
THE KING'S FALCON. Bradbury Press, 1969; London, Macmillan, 1970.

PORTRAIT OF IVAN. Bradbury Press, 1969; London, Macmillan, 1970.

HUNGRY FRED. Bradbury Press, 1969.

BLOWFISH LIVE IN THE SEA. Bradbury Press, 1970; London, Macmillan, 1972.

GOOD ETHAN. Bradbury Press, 1973.

THE SLAVE DANCER. Bradbury Press, 1973; London, Macmillan, 1974.

THE LITTLE SWINEHERD AND OTHER TALES. Dutton, 1978; Dent, 1979.

Leon Garfield

JACK HOLBORN. Kestrel, 1964; Pantheon, 1965.

DEVIL-IN-THE-FOG. Kestrel, 1966; Pantheon, 1966.

SMITH. Kestrel, 1967; Pantheon, 1967.

BLACK JACK. Kestrel, 1968; Pantheon, 1969.

MISTER CORBETT'S GHOST. Pantheon, 1968.

MISTER CORBETT'S GHOST AND OTHER STORIES. Kestrel, 1969.

THE RESTLESS GHOST: THREE STORIES. Pantheon, 1969.

THE DRUMMER BOY. Kestrel, 1970; Pantheon, 1970.

THE BOY AND THE MONKEY. Heinemann, 1969; Watts, 1970.

THE GOD BENEATH THE SEA. (with Edward Blishen). Kestrel, 1970; Pantheon, 1971.

THE STRANGE AFFAIR OF ADELAIDE HARRIS. Kestrel, 1971; Pantheon, 1971.

THE CAPTAIN'S WATCH. Heinemann, 1972.

THE GHOST DOWNSTAIRS. Kestrel, 1972; Pantheon, 1972.

THE GOLDEN SHADOW (with Edward Blishen). Kestrel, 1973; Pantheon, 1973.

LUCIFER WILKINS. Heinemann, 1973.

THE SOUND OF COACHES. Kestrel, 1974; Viking, 1974.

THE PRISONERS OF SEPTEMBER. Kestrel, 1975; Viking, 1975.

THE PLEASURE GARDEN. Kestrel, 1976; Viking, 1976.

*MIRROR, MIRROR. Heinemann, 1976.

*THE LAMPLIGHTER'S FUNERAL. Heinemann, 1976.

*THE CLOAK. Heinemann. 1976.

*MOSS AND BLISTER. Heinemann, 1976.

*THE DUMB CAKE. Heinemann, 1977.

*TOM TITMARSH'S DEVIL. Heinemann, 1977.

Author Bibliographies

*THE FOOL. Heinemann, 1977.
*ROSY STARLING. Heinemann, 1977.
*THE VALENTINE. Heinemann, 1977.
*LABOUR IN VAIN. Heinemann, 1977.
*THE ENEMY. Heinemann, 1978.
*THE FILTHY BEAST. Heinemann, 1978.
THE CONFIDENCE MAN. Kestrel, 1978.
BOSTOCK AND HARRIS. Kestrel, 1979.

*All twelve stories published in one volume as THE APPRENTICES. Viking, 1978.

Alan Garner

THE WEIRDSTONE OF BRISINGAMEN. Collins, 1960; Watts, 1961; new edition Collins World, 1979.
THE MOON OF GOMRATH. Collins, 1963; Walck, 1967; new edition Collins World, 1979.
ELIDOR. Collins, 1965; Walck, 1967.
HOLLY FROM THE BONGS. Collins, 1966.
THE OLD MAN OF MOW. Collins, 1967; Doubleday, 1970.
THE OWL SERVICE. Collins, 1967; Walck, 1968; new edition Collins World, 1979.
RED SHIFT. Collins, 1973; New York, Macmillan, 1973.
THE BREADHORSE. Collins, 1975.
THE GUIZER: A BOOK OF FOOLS. Hamish Hamilton, 1975; Morrow, 1976.
THE STONE BOOK. Collins, 1976; Collins World, 1978.
TOM FOBBLE'S DAY. Collins, 1977; Collins World, 1979.
GRANNY REARDUN. Collins, 1977; Collins World, 1978.
THE AIMER GATE. Collins, 1978; Collins World, 1979.

Virginia Hamilton

ZEELY. New York, Macmillan, 1967.
THE HOUSE OF DIES DREAR. New York, Macmillan, 1968.
THE TIME-AGO TALES OF JAHDU. New York, Macmillan, 1969.
THE PLANET OF JUNIOR BROWN. New York, Macmillan, 1971.
TIME-AGO LOST: MORE TALES OF JAHDU. New York, Macmillan, 1973.

M. C. HIGGINS THE GREAT. New York, Macmillan, 1974; Hamish Hamilton, 1975.

ARILLA SUN DOWN. Morrow, 1976; Hamish Hamilton, 1977.

JUSTICE AND HER BROTHERS. Greenwillow, 1978; Hamish Hamilton, 1979.

E. L. Konigsburg

FROM THE MIXED-UP FILES OF MRS. BASIL E. FRANKWEILER. Atheneum, 1967; London, Macmillan, 1969.

JENNIFER, HECATE, MACBETH, WILLIAM MCKINLEY AND ME, ELIZABETH. Atheneum, 1967; London, Macmillan, 1968, as JENNIFER, HECATE, MACBETH AND ME.

ABOUT THE B'NAI BAGELS. Atheneum, 1969.

(GEORGE). Atheneum, 1970; London, Macmillan, 1971.

ALTOGETHER, ONE AT A TIME. Atheneum, 1971.

A PROUD TASTE FOR SCARLET AND MINIVER. Atheneum, 1973; London, Macmillan, 1974.

THE DRAGON IN THE GHETTO CAPER. Atheneum, 1974; London, Macmillan, 1979.

THE SECOND MRS GIOCONDA. Atheneum, 1975; London, Macmillan, 1976.

FATHER'S ARCANE DAUGHTER. Atheneum, 1976; London, Macmillan, 1977.

Penelope Lively

ASTERCOTE. Heinemann, 1970; Dutton, 1971.

THE WHISPERING KNIGHTS. Heinemann, 1971; Dutton, 1976.

THE WILD HUNT OF HAGWORTHY. Heinemann, 1971; Dutton, 1972, as THE WILD HUNT OF THE GHOST HOUNDS.

THE DRIFTWAY. Heinemann, 1972; Dutton, 1973.

THE GHOST OF THOMAS KEMPE. Heinemann, 1973; Dutton, 1973.

THE HOUSE IN NORHAM GARDENS. Heinemann, 1974; Dutton, 1974.

GOING BACK. Heinemann, 1975; Dutton, 1975.

BOY WITHOUT A NAME. Heinemann, 1975; Parnassus Press, 1975.

Author Bibliographies

THE PRESENCE OF THE PAST: AN INTRODUCTION TO LANDSCAPE HISTORY. Collins, 1976.
A STITCH IN TIME. Heinemann, 1976; Dutton, 1976.
THE STAINED GLASS WINDOW. Abelard-Schuman, 1976.
FANNY'S SISTER. Heinemann, 1977; Dutton, 1979.
THE VOYAGE OF QV 66. Heinemann, 1978; Dutton, 1979.

William Mayne

FOLLOW THE FOOTPRINTS. Oxford University Press, 1953.
THE WORLD UPSIDE DOWN. Oxford University Press, 1954.
A SWARM IN MAY. Oxford University Press, 1955; Bobbs Merrill, 1955.
THE MEMBER FOR THE MARSH. Oxford University Press, 1956.
CHORISTERS' CAKE. Oxford University Press, 1956; Bobbs Merrill, 1958.
THE BLUE BOAT. Oxford University Press, 1957; Dutton, 1960.
A GRASS ROPE. Oxford University Press, 1957; Dutton, 1962.
THE LONG NIGHT. Blackwell, 1958.
UNDERGROUND ALLEY. Oxford University Press, 1958; Dutton, 1961.
THE GOBBLING BILLY (with Dick Caesar, as Dynely James). Gollancz, 1959; Dutton, 1959.
THE THUMBSTICK. Oxford University Press, 1959.
THIRTEEN O'CLOCK. Blackwell, 1960.
THE ROLLING SEASON. Oxford University Press, 1960.
CATHEDRAL WEDNESDAY. Oxford University Press, 1960.
THE FISHING PARTY. Hamish Hamilton, 1960.
SUMMER VISITORS. Oxford University Press, 1961.
THE CHANGELING. Oxford University Press, 1961; Dutton, 1963.
THE GLASS BALL. Hamish Hamilton, 1961; Dutton, 1962.
THE LAST BUS. Hamish Hamilton, 1962.
THE TWELVE DANCERS. Hamish Hamilton, 1962.
THE MAN FROM THE NORTH POLE. Hamish Hamilton, 1963.
ON THE STEPPING STONES. Hamish Hamilton, 1963.
WORDS AND MUSIC. Hamish Hamilton, 1963.
PLOT NIGHT. Hamish Hamilton, 1963; Dutton, 1968.
A PARCEL OF TREES. Hamish Hamilton, 1964.
WATER BOATMAN. Hamish Hamilton, 1964.

WHISTLING RUFUS. Hamish Hamilton, 1964; Dutton, 1965.
SAND. Hamish Hamilton, 1964; Dutton, 1965.
A DAY WITHOUT WIND. Hamish Hamilton, 1964; Dutton, 1964.
THE BIG WHEEL AND THE LITTLE WHEEL. Hamish Hamilton, 1965.
PIG IN THE MIDDLE. Hamish Hamilton, 1965; Dutton, 1966.
NO MORE SCHOOL. Hamish Hamilton, 1965.
DORMOUSE TALES (as Charles Molin). Hamish Hamilton, 1966.
EARTHFASTS. Hamish Hamilton, 1966; Dutton, 1967.
ROOFTOPS. Hamish Hamilton, 1966.
THE OLD ZION. Hamish Hamilton, 1966; Dutton, 1967.
THE BATTLEFIELD. Hamish Hamilton, 1967; Dutton, 1967.
THE BIG EGG. Hamish Hamilton, 1967.
THE TOFFEE JOIN. Hamish Hamilton, 1968.
OVER THE HILLS AND FAR AWAY. Hamish Hamilton, 1968; Dutton, 1969, as THE HILL ROAD.
THE YELLOW AEROPLANE. Hamish Hamilton, 1968; Nelson, 1974.
THE HOUSE ON FAIRMOUNT. Hamish Hamilton, 1968; Dutton, 1968.
RAVENSGILL. Hamish Hamilton, 1970; Dutton, 1970.
ROYAL HARRY. Hamish Hamilton, 1971; Dutton, 1972.
A GAME OF DARK. Hamish Hamilton, 1971; Dutton, 1971.
THE INCLINE. Hamish Hamilton, 1972; Dutton, 1972.
THE SWALLOWS (as Martin Cobalt). Heinemann, 1972; Nelson, 1974, as POOL OF SWALLOWS.
ROBIN'S REAL ENGINE. Hamish Hamilton, 1972.
SKIFFY. Hamish Hamilton, 1972.
THE JERSEY SHORE. Hamish Hamilton, 1973; Dutton, 1973.
A YEAR AND A DAY. Hamish Hamilton, 1976; Dutton, 1976.
PARTY PANTS. Hodder & Stoughton, 1977.
MAX'S DREAM. Hamish Hamilton, 1977.
IT. Hamish Hamilton, 1977; Greenwillow, 1978.

Jill Paton Walsh

HENGEST'S TALE. London, Macmillan, 1966; St Martin's Press, 1966.
THE DOLPHIN CROSSING. London, Macmillan, 1967; St Martin's Press, 1967.

Author Bibliographies

WORDHOARD: ANGLO-SAXON STORIES (with Kevin Crossley-Holland). London, Macmillan, 1969; Farrar Straus, 1975.

FIREWEED. London, Macmillan, 1969; Farrar Straus, 1970.

GOLDENGROVE. London, Macmillan, 1972; Farrar Straus, 1972.

THE DAWNSTONE. Hamish Hamilton, 1973.

TOOLMAKER. Heinemann, 1973; Seabury Press, 1974.

THE EMPEROR'S WINDING SHEET. London, Macmillan, 1974; Farrar Straus, 1974.

THE BUTTY BOY. London, Macmillan, 1975; Farrar Straus, 1975, as THE HUFFLER.

THE ISLAND SUNRISE: PREHISTORIC CULTURE IN THE BRITISH ISLES. André Deutsch, 1975; Seabury Press, 1976.

UNLEAVING. London, Macmillan, 1976; Farrar Straus, 1976.

*THE WALLS OF ATHENS. Heinemann, 1977.

*CROSSING TO SALAMIS. Heinemann, 1977.

*PERSIAN GOLD. Heinemann, 1978.

A CHANCE CHILD. London, Macmillan, 1978; Farrar Strauss, 1978.

*All three stories published in one volume as CHILDREN OF THE FOX. Farrar Straus, 1978.

K. M. Peyton

SABRE, THE HORSE FROM THE SEA (as Kathleen Herald). A. & C. Black, 1948; New York, Macmillan, 1963.

THE MANDRAKE (as Kathleen Herald). A. & C. Black, 1949.

CRAB THE ROAN (as Kathleen Herald). A. & C. Black, 1953.

NORTH TO ADVENTURE. Collins, 1958; Platt & Munk, 1965.

STORMCOCK MEETS TROUBLE. Collins, 1961.

THE HARD WAY HOME. Collins, 1962; Platt & Munk, 1964, as SING A SONG OF AMBUSH.

WINDFALL. Oxford University Press, 1962; World, 1963, as SEA FEVER.

BROWNSEA SILVER. Collins, 1964.

THE MAPLIN BIRD. Oxford University Press, 1964; World, 1965.

THE PLAN FOR BIRDSMARSH. Oxford University Press, 1965; World, 1966.

THUNDER IN THE SKY. Oxford University Press, 1966; World, 1967.

FLAMBARDS. Oxford University Press, 1967; World, 1968.

FLY-BY-NIGHT. Oxford University Press, 1968; World, 1969.

THE EDGE OF THE CLOUD. Oxford University Press, 1969; World, 1970.

FLAMBARDS IN SUMMER. Oxford University Press, 1969; World, 1970.

PENNINGTON'S SEVENTEENTH SUMMER. Oxford University Press, 1970; Crowell, 1971, as PENNINGTON'S LAST TERM.

THE BEETHOVEN MEDAL. Oxford University Press, 1971; Crowell, 1972.

A PATTERN OF ROSES. Oxford University Press, 1972; Crowell, 1973.

PENNINGTON'S HEIR. Oxford University Press, 1973; Crowell, 1974.

THE TEAM. Oxford University Press, 1975; Crowell, 1976.

THE RIGHT-HAND MAN. Oxford University Press, 1977.

PROVE YOURSELF A HERO. Oxford University Press, 1977; Collins World, 1978.

A MIDSUMMER NIGHT'S DEATH. Oxford University Press, 1978; Collins World, 1979.

Ivan Southall

MEET SIMON BLACK. Angus & Robertson, 1950.

SIMON BLACK IN PERIL. Angus & Robertson, 1951.

SIMON BLACK IN SPACE. Angus & Robertson, 1952.

SIMON BLACK IN COASTAL COMMAND. Angus & Robertson, 1953.

SIMON BLACK IN CHINA. Angus & Robertson, 1954.

SIMON BLACK AND THE SPACEMEN. Angus & Robertson, 1955.

SIMON BLACK IN THE ANTARCTIC. Angus & Robertson, 1956.

SIMON BLACK TAKES OVER. Angus & Robertson, 1959.

SIMON BLACK AT SEA. Angus & Robertson, 1961.

JOURNEY INTO MYSTERY: A STORY OF THE EXPLORERS BURKE AND WILLS. Lansdowne Press, 1961.

HILLS END. Angus & Robertson, 1962; St Martin's Press, 1963.

LAWRENCE HARGRAVE. Melbourne, Oxford University Press, 1964.

INDONESIAN JOURNEY. Lansdowne Press, 1965; Ginn, 1966.

Author Bibliographies

ROCKETS IN THE DESERT: THE STORY OF WOOMERA. Angus & Robertson, 1965.

ASH ROAD. Angus & Robertson, 1965; St Martin's Press, 1966.

THE FOX HOLE. Methuen, 1967; St Martin's Press, 1967.

THE SWORD OF ESAU: BIBLE STORIES RETOLD. Angus & Robertson, 1967; St Martin's Press, 1968.

TO THE WILD SKY. Angus & Robertson, 1967; St Martin's Press, 1967.

BUSHFIRE! Angus & Robertson, 1968.

THE CURSE OF CAIN: BIBLE STORIES RETOLD. Angus & Robertson, 1968; St Martin's Press, 1968.

SLY OLD WARDROBE. Cheshire-Angus & Robertson, 1968; St Martin's Press, 1969.

LET THE BALLOON GO. Methuen, 1968; St Martin's Press, 1968.

FINN'S FOLLY. Angus & Robertson, 1969; St Martin's Press, 1969.

CHINAMAN'S REEF IS OURS. Angus & Robertson, 1970; St Martin's Press, 1970.

BREAD AND HONEY. Angus & Robertson, 1970; Bradbury Press, 1970, as WALK A MILE AND GET NOWHERE.

JOSH. Angus & Robertson, 1971; New York, Macmillan, 1972.

OVER THE TOP. Methuen, 1972; New York, Macmillan, 1973, as BENSON BOY.

HEAD IN THE CLOUDS. Angus & Robertson, 1972; New York, Macmillan, 1973.

MATT AND JO. Angus & Robertson, 1974; New York, Macmillan, 1973.

SEVENTEEN SECONDS. Hodder & Stoughton, 1973; New York, Macmillan, 1974.

FLY WEST. Angus & Robertson, 1974; New York, Macmillan, 1975.

WHAT ABOUT TOMORROW? Angus & Robertson, 1977; New York, Macmillan, 1977.

KING OF THE STICKS. William Collins (Australia), 1979; Methuen, 1979; Greenwillow, 1979.

Patricia Wrightson

THE CROOKED SNAKE. Angus & Robertson, 1955; Hutchinson, 1973.

THE BUNYIP HOLE. Angus & Robertson, 1958; Hutchinson, 1973.

THE ROCKS OF HONEY. Angus & Robertson, 1960.

THE FEATHER STAR. Hutchinson, 1962; Harcourt Brace, 1963.

DOWN TO EARTH. Hutchinson, 1965; Harcourt Brace, 1965.

'I OWN THE RACECOURSE!'. Hutchinson, 1968; Harcourt Brace, 1968, as A RACECOURSE FOR ANDY.

AN OLDER KIND OF MAGIC. Hutchinson, 1972; Harcourt Brace, 1972.

THE NARGUN AND THE STARS. Hutchinson, 1973; Atheneum, 1974.

THE ICE IS COMING. Hutchinson, 1977; Atheneum, 1977.

John Rowe Townsend

GUMBLE'S YARD. Hutchinson, 1961; Lippincott, 1969, as TROUBLE IN THE JUNGLE.

HELL'S EDGE. Hutchinson, 1963; Lothrop, 1969.

WIDDERSHINS CRESCENT. Hutchinson, 1965; Lippincott, 1967, as GOOD-BYE TO THE JUNGLE.

THE HALLERSAGE SOUND. Hutchinson, 1966.

PIRATE'S ISLAND. Oxford University Press, 1968; Lippincott, 1968.

THE INTRUDER. Oxford University Press, 1969; Lippincott, 1970.

GOODNIGHT, PROF, LOVE. Oxford University Press, 1970; Lippincott, 1971, as GOODNIGHT, PROF, DEAR.

THE SUMMER PEOPLE. Oxford University Press, 1972; Lippincott, 1972.

A WISH FOR WINGS. Heinemann, 1972.

FOREST OF THE NIGHT. Oxford University Press, 1974; Lippincott, 1975.

NOAH'S CASTLE. Oxford University Press, 1975; Lippincott, 1976.

TOP OF THE WORLD. Oxford University Press, 1976; Lippincott, 1977.

THE XANADU MANUSCRIPT. Oxford University Press, 1977; Lippincott, 1977, as THE VISITORS.